THE GREATEST SALES STORIES EVER TOLD

THE GREATEST SALES STORIES EVER TOLD

From the World's Best Salespeople

Robert L. Shook

McGraw-Hill, Inc.
New York   San Francisco   Washington, D.C.   Auckland   Bogotá
Caracas   Lisbon   London   Madrid   Mexico City   Milan
Montreal   New Delhi   San Juan   Singapore
Sydney   Tokyo   Toronto

Library of Congress Cataloging-in-Publication Data

Shook, Robert L.
    The greatest sales stories ever told, from the world's best
salespeople / Robert L. Shook
        p.   cm.
    Includes index
    ISBN 0-07-057134-1 (Hardcover)
    1. Selling.   2. Selling—Case studies. I. Title
. HF5438.25.S54   1995
   658.85—dc20   95-18150
                                          CIP

1 2 3 4 5 6 7 8 9 0 DOC/DOC 9 0 0 9 8 7 6 5

ISBN 0-07-057134-1

*The sponsoring editor for this book was Philip Ruppel, the editing supervisor
was Paul R. Sobel, and the production supervisor was Suzanne W. B.
Rapcavage. It was set in Fairfield by Dina E. John of McGraw-Hill's
Professional Book Group composition unit.*

Printed and bound by R. R. Donnelley & Sons Company.

McGraw-Hill books are available at special quantity discounts to use as
premiums and sales promotions, or for use in corporate training programs.
For more information, please write to the Director of Special Sales,
McGraw-Hill, Inc., 11 West 19th Street, New York, NY 10011. Or contact
your local bookstore.

This book is dedicated with love to my son, RJ

CONTENTS

INTRODUCTION

Now and then people ask me where I get my book ideas. The seed was planted for *The Greatest Sales Stories Ever Told* long before I ever dreamed about a writing career. It occurred in the early 1960s when I was pounding the pavement as a young rookie salesman.

Some of my best times during my early sales career were when I was around a group of seasoned sales pros, listening to them swap stories about their greatest and most spectacular sales. I loved hearing them talk about how one got his foot in the door of a particularly hard-nosed prospect, how somebody else closed an incredibly difficult sale, and how still another had a particularly tough customer who became the best-ever source for his referrals—the stories went on and on.

Not only did I love these tales—*through them I learned so much about selling.* I often thought I would enjoy reading a book filled with such stories. At the time, it never dawned on me that I'd be its author.

Today, as a salesperson-turned-writer, I've interviewed hundreds of salespeople, including many of the world's number one producers, in diverse fields ranging from insurance to securities and from real estate to computers. Invariably each superstar has a favorite story to tell. Now after having written three dozen books, I am finally writing that collection of wonderful sales stories.

For including a story, my criteria were two. It must be entertaining. The market is already saturated with how-to-sell books—so unless I could write something truly unique, adding to the staid list of published sales material has no appeal to me.

My intent, however, is not solely to entertain you. Each story must also have a moral or a lesson to enhance your selling skills.

Each story illustrates how a sale was made as a result of something specific the individual thought, said, or did—something you can do too! So while you will enjoy reading these stories, don't be too eager to scoot on to the next story; first, digest the message of the story you just read. Learn its lesson. Analyze it. And figure out how to apply it to what you sell.

Remember too that most salespeople exchange ideas only with other salespeople in their respective fields. Rarely, for example, does an insurance agent swap ideas with a computer company representative. But I long ago discovered that some of the best ideas are those "borrowed" from another industry—they are particularly effective because they offer fresh approaches versus those that have become stale from being overworked by the same salespeople competing directly against one another for the same business. So I implore you not to pass over ideas from salespeople outside your field. Instead, try to analyze what they do, and with some intelligent application, make it transferable to what you sell.

Each is a true story and contains a lesson that has been field-tested—what you learn in this book *truly works in the real world!* While interviewing scores of salespeople during my research for this book, I also recalled several incidents about my own personal selling experiences. I could not resist—some of my own stories are sprinkled throughout these pages.

As you turn the pages of this book, you will meet some of America's most interesting people. Included are Rich Luisi, Electrolux's number one vacuum sweeper salesperson for five consecutive years. And there is Barry Kaye, a super life insurance agent who sells multi-million dollar policies to America's most rich and famous. You will also read about Stan Herman, a highly successful Beverly Hills Realtor who has made a fortune selling multi-million-dollar homes to people in the entertainment industry. And you will be introduced to Bill Bresnan, former CEO of Teleprompter. Bill tells a wonderful story about how a "lost" sale was turned around in a bid for a cable television franchise that, over the years, has produced profits into nine figures. There are other people with whom you are already familiar, men and women who started off as salespeople, and who as a result of their phenomenal selling success, rose to become household names in America. For instance, you'll meet presidential candidate and billionaire Ross Perot, and Mary Kay Ash, founder of Mary Kay Cosmetics. Other stories feature individuals whose names you may not recognize, but whose company names are certainly household names, such as William Chaney, CEO of Tiffany's, and Isadore Sharp, founder and CEO of Four Seasons Hotels. These people tell wonderful stories about their sales careers during the days when they were making calls on customers—spending every day in the field—just like you may do today. It doesn't matter what you sell, you will love reading these stories as told by some of the gretest salespeople ever.

All the techniques that work like a charm in these stories will work for you because the principles of selling are constant, whether you are selling vacuum sweepers, $10,000,000 life insurance policies, million-dollar homes, or multi-million-dollar computer systems. So sit back and enjoy these stories as they are intended to be enjoyed. When you do, you'll learn the important principles they teach. And now if I may put on my hat as an ex-salesperson, at the risk of puffing my own sails or beating on my own chest—*you are in for a real treat*. This I can assure you with complete confidence—because I know how much I personally enjoyed hearing these stories as they were told to me!

Robert L. Shook

ACKNOWLEDGMENTS

My special thanks goes to the wonderful storytellers in this book who graciously shared their stories with me. For obvious reasons, without them, this book would have never been written. Some of these people were already good friends of mine; and while conducting interviews for this book, I made some new friends—*what a great bonus!*

Maggie Abel, my assistant, did a superb job in both her transcribing and editing work. She also served as a good sounding board for ideas—her feedback was very much appreciated. (Maggie, I never stop appreciating you.)

As always, my agent, Al Zuckerman, President of Writers House, believed in this project from start to finish. When you read this book, Al appears in my storytelling—and you'll see why I think he is America's finest literary agent (an opinion shared by many professional writers). Once again, Al, thank you for everything you do for my writing career—and for being my good friend.

Finally, I am grateful to two highly talented individuals at McGraw-Hill, Inc. Paul Sobel who did an exceptional job as the book's senior editing supervisor, and Philip Ruppel, publisher, for his role in publishing this book. I have worked with Philip on previous books, so I had good reason to seek him out for this publication. Philip, it's a pleasure and a privilege to work with a person of your calibre.

MENTAL ATTITUDE

E very sale begins in the mind of a salesperson. Before you can
sell anything to anybody, you must first believe that you
will make the sale. If you don't believe in yourself, your company,
and your product, it is unlikely that you will ever convince anybody
else to believe in it either. In this first part, you will learn
how having a positive mental attitude is essential in the selling
process.

SELLING WITH ENTHUSIASM

Told by Mary Kay Ash

When I was a young housewife, late one Friday afternoon, my doorbell rang. Ida Blake, someone I had never met, stood at my door asking if she could come in to explain the merits of owning a set of books to read to young children. I invited her in, and before I knew it, she had me completely sold on her product, the *Child Psychology Bookshelf*, published by Grolier's Society. A mother could look up any problem in the index, and find a related story with a good moral to read to her child.

For instance, one story dealt with a child who told fibs— which children sometimes do at ages four and five. As a young mother trying to teach my children the difference between right and wrong, I thought those books were the best I'd ever seen.

When Ida told me the books cost $50, tears came to my eyes. "I'm sorry, but I could no more buy them than fly to the moon," I told her. "They're way out of my league."

Ida could see I loved them, so she said, "Mary Kay, suppose I leave them with you and pick them up on Monday. Is that okay?"

"That's wonderful," I told her, "but there's no point in it, because there's no way I can afford them."

"I'll tell you what," she said. "You sell 10 sets for me and I'll give you a set."

"Really? Gee, that's wonderful," I said with a faint smile.

At the time, I was volunteer superintendent of the beginners' Sunday School program at Houston's Tabernacle Baptist Church, so I had the phone numbers of many mothers. I spent much of that weekend on the telephone calling up these mothers, telling them about the best books I'd ever seen. My enthusiasm was such that without even showing the books to anyone, I was able to sell 10 sets—sight unseen! What happened was, I got so excited that the women got excited too.

When Ida came back Monday morning, I told her what I had done. "Here are their names and addresses," I said. "All you have to do is go out and pick up their money."

"This is incredible! I've never seen anything like this," she said. "That's your set to keep, Mary Kay," she said, pointing at the books on my dining room table.

"Oh, thank you," I answered with a lump in my throat.

"Now, I've got something more important to discuss with you, Mary Kay." Ida sounded excited. "How would you like to sell for our company?" Without waiting for an answer, she added, "By the way, you'll need a car."

"We have one car and my husband takes it to work. Besides, I don't know how to drive," I said.

"You tell your husband to leave you the car, and I'll take you out in it tomorrow. And, honey, you and I are going to sell some books!"

The following day we spent knocking on doors, but we either found no one home or got the door slammed in our faces. At the end of the day, we hadn't made a single sale. Not one person was interested. I couldn't get over it—I had sold 10 sets over the weekend on the telephone, and now Ida was having so much trouble.

At 5 p.m., Ida climbed into the passenger's side of the car and announced, "You're driving home."

"But I can't drive," I cried.

"If you're going to be a saleswoman, you've got to learn some-time," she said philosophically. That day I received my first driving lesson—traveling through Houston during rush hour in bumper-to-bumper traffic.

So, thanks to Ida, I not only landed my first sales job, I learned how to drive a car.

I didn't know much about selling, but I saw little hope of succeeding by duplicating Ida's cold calls and door-to-door canvassing. I figured I had been able to sell those 10 sets of books because of my enthusiasm for them.

I immediately got a list of Baptist parents who had children in the Houston area and started making appointments. I sold $25,000 worth of books during my first nine months, making me one of the company's top salespeople. In spite of this, I decided to quit. My reason was calls I received from irate parents! You see, some parents invested $50 in the books, let them just sit on the shelf, and then got mad at me because they didn't work. Of course, had the books been used properly, my customers would have definitely received their money's worth.

Knowing that my customers weren't using the books soured me on selling them. I had lost my enthusiasm, and without it, I didn't have the heart to sell those books!

Anyone who has ever met Mary Kay Ash knows just how contagious her enthusiasm is. You simply can't help but feel it when you're in her presence. Enthusiasm works this way for every salesperson. When you believe in what you sell—heart and soul—others are bound to feel the same way!

Mary Kay Ash left the book business, and years later in 1963, she started her own company, Mary Kay Cosmetics. Today, she is considered one of America's most successful businesswomen. Headquartered in Dallas, Mary Kay Cosmetics has an estimated 375,000 beauty consultants with an estimated $2 billion in retail sales each year. Known today as "Mary Kay Enthusiasm," Ms. Ash's enthusiasm has become legendary.

THE BIGGER THEY (PROSPECTS) ARE

Told by Jack A. Sullivan

In 1977, at age 30, after being in the securities business for eight years, I took a leave of absence with no definite length of time in mind. It turned out to be a five-year sabbatical. When I finally got back into the business, it was at the beginning of the bull market that started in August 1983, and the initial public offering (IPO) market was red hot.

Companies with new offerings were continually coming to town with their road shows to make their pitch to the San Francisco investment community, and with so many meetings going on, it was virtually impossible to attend all of them. However, I didn't have much going on at the time, so I'd go to these meetings, and afterward, I would put together reports on the companies that impressed me. I then distributed them to institutional investors that I felt were good prospects.

During these IPO meetings, I met with the top executives of the company and also took the opportunity to get to know some institutional buyers. Attending IPO meetings was a very efficient way to research a company. In 90 minutes or so I was able to get an in-depth crash course on a company's business, finances, management, competition, and prospects for future growth.

About 100 people would generally be present and often there was standing room only. At one such meeting, however, the entire audience consisted of the chairman of the presenting company, the chief financial officer, two representatives with L.F. Rothchild & Co. (the underwriting brokerage firm), and yours truly. This was a time when the high-tech stocks from Silicon Valley were at their pinnacle, and this particular offering was for the ultimate low-tech stock, Agency Rent-A-Car. It was a little company from Cleveland, Ohio that dealt in rental cars, not chips. The company dominated the insurance replacement field, an industry that cars rented to insurance company clients whose cars had been in an accident or stolen.

If they looked at it at all, I suppose most investors looked at Agency as just another rental car company that would be competing against Hertz, Avis, and the rest of the big guys. But I discovered at the meeting that just the opposite was true. I became enamored with the company's story when I found out how much sense its business made. Unlike the bigger car rental companies, Agency Rent-A-Car didn't need an airport or downtown location, nor did it have to remain open 24 hours a day, seven days a week. The company's hours were 9 to 5, and it towed each car to the renter's house—all for $13 a day versus the rental giants' $21 plus. Almost all its customers came from insurance companies' referrals, and thus it had no real competition except for some scattered regional mom-and-pop organizations.

I thought the company was a win-win situation. It had everything going for it but investors. Everybody either hated it or ignored it. The company simply had no sex appeal. When I got back to my office, I reviewed my notes and wrote them out. I thought to myself: "Here is a company with a compellingly low valuation, hands-on management, and vast growth potential. Besides being attractive, the company is unique. It dominates a very lucrative industry, management is extremely focused, and, critical to my way of thinking, they owned almost all the shares themselves. Somebody is going to buy this stock. But while this is a tremendous company, if the reception that Agency Rent-A-Car received in San Francisco was any indication, the stock is going to be inefficiently priced. I considered that very good news."

I started wondering to myself who would appreciate this company. I thought and thought. Then I remembered an article I read about the types of stocks bought for America's largest mutual fund, the Fidelity Magellan fund. Peter Lynch, the legendary manager of the fund, placed a great deal of weight on small-cap stocks, using them as a barometer for developing industries. During his 13-year tenure, Lynch was overwhelmingly successful, having returned 2703 percent to investors. Lynch was the most famous fund manager in the world. He was the fellow with the most assets under management and the largest number of stocks. Everything about his operation was the biggest and the best and the most.

So I dialed Fidelity's number, and admittedly, I was nervous when I asked the operator, "May I please have Peter Lynch's number?"

I dialed the number and instead of going through a battery of secretaries as I anticipated, a voice answered, "Peter Lynch speaking."

"My name is Jack Sullivan," I said, "and you don't know me and you don't know my firm." (I was with an independent broker with a small firm that no longer exists.) "But I just saw a company that you should be interested in...."

There was no response and, quite frankly, I was stunned that I had got put through so easily to Peter Lynch. "Now you may not want to hear this," I continued.

"No, go ahead, go ahead," he replied.

"Well, at the IPO lunch for Agency Rent-A-Car here in San Francisco, I saw what I believe is an enormously attractive company. Surprisingly, I was the only person in the room except for the underwriter and the management. I think you have an opportunity here to buy a lot of something that is going to be priced very inefficiently. They will be in Boston on Thursday."

"Why do you like it?" Lynch asked.

Then I briefly highlighted a few of the best reasons to own the stock.

"Thank you. Goodbye." He hung up.

Several months went by, and I saw another company that I liked, so once again I decided to call Lynch. And again, he answered the phone directly.

"This is Jack Sullivan calling...."

Before I could say anything else, he answered, "Oh, good, it's you. I bought a couple hundred thousand shares of the stock you recommended. That was a great idea. I can use someone like you."

It was Napoleon who said, "Men will die for ribbons," and all I needed was somebody like Peter Lynch to say, "I could use somebody like you." His words were a tremendous boost to me. This incident confirmed that I could be a factor if not a force in the business. It legitimized the entire concept of my business strategy of looking for inefficiently priced situations. I realized that I could contribute and make a difference in the business lives of people managing major money.

Incidentally, Agency Rent-A-Car came out at 4, and at an adjusted price for stock splits climbed to 19. Needless to say, Peter Lynch was happy with its performance, and afterward we did a lot of business until he retired in 1990. To this day, I still work with Fidelity.

Jack Sullivan says that once he gained Fidelity as a client, his confidence level soared. "It gave me the courage of my convictions," he states, "and I realized that I could call on anybody. I also knew I could pick stocks." After his success with Peter Lynch, Jack Sullivan continued to make many more calls on other high-profile institutional prospects and wealthy investors; he has since become one of the nation's most successful stockbrokers. This story reveals how renowned, affluent people are approachable—and that is one of the reasons they are at the top! Because they are willing to listen to new ideas, they frequently make themselves available to salespeople. (Also remember that many people at this level are sales-driven and therefore more receptive to salespeople.)

Jack A. Sullivan was graduated from Georgetown University in 1969 and started his career in the securities industry with a small brokerage firm in New York City. One year later, he purchased his own seat on the American Stock Exchange and began trading his own account and executing trades for firms that specialized in what was then the fairly new business of institutional investing. In 1974, he moved from his native New Jersey to San Francisco and today is a principal with Van Kasper & Company. He deals with a select number of institutional clients across the United States and Europe; he also manages individual accounts on a discretionary basis.

SELLING MULTI-MILLION DOLLAR HOMES IN BEVERLY HILLS

Told by Stan Herman

In 1976, the estate of the famous comedian and actor Harold Lloyd was put on the market. Lloyd was one of Hollywood's most famous comedian/actors, and although some people don't recognize his name today, practically everybody is familiar with the guy in one of Hollywood's most classic scenes who is hanging from the clock. That's Harold Lloyd.

Built in the late 1920s, the Lloyd property was a legendary Beverly Hills house that sat on 15.77 acres of prime property adjoining movie mogul Jack Warner's estate. Warner owned nine acres, and between the two of them, they shared an 18-hole golf course. Every Sunday Lloyd's pub room was filled with scores of the movie industry's most glamorous people, including many beautiful wives and girlfriends, who would assemble to watch the men play golf. For many Hollywood hopefuls, it was the place to be on Sunday afternoons during the 1930s and 1940s.

The house was a landmark, so when Lloyd died and the word

got out that it was put on the market, everyone anticipated a record-breaking sale. At the time, as the broker of oil magnate Arthur Cameron's estate, I held the record for being the real estate broker who made the first million-dollar sale in the entire area. Like many other Beverly Hills real estate people, I wanted to be the selling broker on this sale. To me, selling the Lloyd estate was simply a matter of pride.

However, I didn't get the listing. In fact, nobody did. The estate trustees hired Milton Wershaw Auctioneers to auction it off, which meant the real estate commissions would be split between Wershaw, an eminent auctioneer in L.A., and the real estate broker. Wershaw Auctioneers were the best in their field and they knew their business quite well. So for good reason, they didn't bother to put a listing price on the Lloyd estate. It wasn't necessary because everyone knew the price would start in the million-dollar range. Having potential buyers bid on it, they determined, would generate the highest price.

It was my good fortune to have Mary Douvan work in my office. As a point of interest, this wonderful little lady is the mother of Sandra Dee, the popular actress back in the 1950s and 1960s. Mary had made excellent contacts with some Iranian buyers to whom she sold several properties. In the mid-1970s, before the Shah of Iran was dethroned, Iranian investors had been pouring a lot of money into California real estate.

At the time the Lloyd estate became available, Mary was working with two Iranian gentlemen. Interestingly, they didn't speak much English, and she spoke to them through a translator. They were crazy about Mary and because the Iranians were private and clannish people, they'd refer many of their friends and associates to her as well as staying with her to buy more real estate. One Saturday afternoon while showing them a shopping center in Santa Barbara, Mary mentioned that the Harold Lloyd estate was coming up for auction the next day. Their eyes lit up when she told them.

"Make arrangements for us to see the Lloyd house," they told her through the interpreter.

With that, they told their driver to immediately take them back to Beverly Hills so they could see the Lloyd estate before the sun went down. They raced back and stormed through the gates of the estate to view the grounds.

As soon as Mary got home, she called me. "Stan, my clients want to attend tomorrow's auction. Set it up for us, okay?" she excitedly asked me. I knew her clients were serious buyers because we had previously sold them a house. There was, however, a minor problem.

As I explained to Mary, "One of the auction's prerequisites is that the buyer must put up a $250,000 cashier's check to accompany the winning bid."

"But the banks are closed over the weekend," she replied. "How do you suggest we get a cashier's check for $250,000 on Sunday?"

"I don't have the slightest idea," I answered. "But I'll come up with something, Mary, so don't you worry about it. You just have your clients at the estate tomorrow at noon and I'll take care of everything else."

The first thing I did was call the interpreter. It was after 9 p.m. and luckily I was able to catch him at home. I explained the terms of the auction and that $250,000 was needed as a down payment by the high bidder.

"I am sorry, Mr. Herman, but we don't have that amount of cash on hand," he said politely.

"Do you have anything else?" I asked.

"Like what?"

"Well, do you have jewelry, diamonds, or perhaps fine art?"

"Not that's available."

"How about cars?" I asked in desperation.

"No," he answered.

"Can you think of anything else you can put up in lieu of cash?"

"No," he answered again.

"Okay," I told him. "Let me work things out. I will see you at the Lloyd estate tomorrow."

It was well after 10 p.m., and I knew I wouldn't be able to sleep if I didn't first get this problem resolved. This was too big a real estate auction for me to be sitting on the sidelines. And knowing that Mary had a good prospect made me determined to come up with a solution so, at the very least, we could be a player at Sunday's auction.

The only thing I could think of was to call the auctioneer at his home. Fortunately, I was able to get through to him. I explained the situation, and as I anticipated, he explained the prerequisite to bidding on the estate was a $250,000 cashier's check.

"I understand," I told him, "and we've been trying to raise the cash, but it's Saturday night and we can't get to a bank until Monday morning."

"How much cash do they have on them?" he asked.

"Oh, something like $10,000 to $20,000 which they brought on their trip for traveling money. However, before you rule them out, let me tell you who these people are. First, I can vouch for them because they already bought a house from my firm. At that particular sale, everything went like clockwork. There were no problems whatsoever. It was an easy, smooth closing.

"Second, these are very honorable people, and may I add, very substantial. I think you would be making a serious mistake if you did not allow them to participate in the auction because of a technicality. These are precisely the types of people whom you want to be at your auction. Their presence will only enhance the sale of the property."

To my surprise, he agreed to waive the mandatory $250,000 cashier's check. I was so excited, I couldn't sleep that night!

About 200 people attended the auction. In fact, it was such an event, there were even television crews. After all, this was one of the major Beverly Hills properties. So there the five of us were. Mary and I were standing with the two Iranians who didn't speak any English and their interpreter.

The first bid was for $1 million, and it kept on going up in increments of $25,000. It quickly went to $1.1 million, then

$1.25 million, and so on until it was $1.4 million. With a crowd of 200, I observed there were only three parties bidding against us. When the bidding reached $1.4 million, only one other bidder remained.

Several years previous, I was told by one of the principals of Aames Auctioneers in Beverly Hills that whenever people bid on something at an auction—whether real estate, art, antiques, or jewelry—their bids are made in specific increments established early on in the auctioning. For instance, if an antique is being auctioned in the $1000 price range, the bidding might increase by $50 or $100 at a time. If it's a museum-quality oil painting in the $10 million range, the bids might go up $100,000 or $200,000 at a time. It is as if there is a magical number that people peg into. Inevitably, the bidding will begin to creep up by a determined increment until there is a time lapse between bids. At this point the pace of the bidding dramatically slows down. I have been told it is precisely then that a smart maneuver is to make a major move by raising your bid at an out-sync increment. Above all else, it lets the competition know you definitely mean business. In addition, you catch the other guy so much off guard that by the time he regroups to figure out his next move, the auction is over.

Having attended many previous auctions, I sensed it was time for my Iranian clients to make such a move. Through the interpreter, I explained that, when the one remaining bidder raised his bid by $25,000 and I gave him a nudge, the Iranians should jump their offer to $1.6 million. Well, I waited until the other guy raised the bid from $1,450,000 to $1,475,000, and then I gave him a swift poke with my elbow.

With that, his arm shot up and he declared, "$1.6 million."

There was a hush, and the auctioneer asked for a first, a second, and a third call. Following a few moments of silence, he announced, "Sold for $1.6 million."

This story has a happy ending for my Iranian clients. Over the years, they divided the 15.77 acres of property surrounding the house into individual lots and reaped more than $40 million.

What's more, during this past year, we sold the Harold Lloyd house, which sat on the remaining lot of about five acres, to a grocery store mogul for $17.5 million.

As you can see, prices have since dwarfed our record sales figure of $1.6 million for a Beverly Hills residential property. By the way, David Geffen, of Geffen Records, recently purchased the Warner estate that adjoined the Lloyd estate. The estate has nine acres and went for $47.5 million—that could be the record for a residential resale in the entire United States!

In this story, the actual sale began when Stan Herman was told that the rules of the auction required a $250,000 cashier's check to be paid upon making the final bid. When Herman was informed that his clients were unable to come up with this amount of cash prior to the auction, he persisted in finding a solution. Lesser salespeople would have given up and said, "Well, there is nothing more I can do. It is just not in the cards for me to participate in this sale. What a shame there wasn't more time for my client to come up with the money. Well, there is always next time."

With a professional salesperson such as Stan Herman, he refused to think negatively and throw in the towel. As a consequence, by making a last-minute call to the auctioneer at his home late on a Saturday night, Herman was able to "make things happen." Then, too, Herman knew there was everything to gain and nothing to lose by trying. Too often, salespeople are fearful about daring to do what is not considered proper protocol. Because they dread the anticipated embarrassment of being called for their faux pas, they never attempt to do what they could have otherwise accomplished. All because they couldn't deal with getting a little slap on the wrist.

Stan Herman has been selling Beverly Hills real estate since 1957. In 1990, his firm Stan Herman & Associates changed its name to Stan Herman, Stephen Shapiro & Associates. Over the years, Herman has handled real estate transactions for many of

Hollywood's biggest stars, including Dan Ackroyd, Stevie Wonder, Barbra Streisand, Gregory Peck, Kenny Rogers, Mick Jagger, Kirk Douglas, Faye Dunaway, Burt Reynolds, Liza Minnelli, Walter Matthau, Harvey Keitel, Prince, Eddie Murphy, Aaron Spelling, Kirk Kerkorian, Ben Vereen, Bill Murray, Debra Winger, Bill Cosby, and Mel Gibson.

WHERE THERE'S A WILL, THERE'S A WAY

Told by Michael McCafferty

St. Patrick's Day 1983 is a date I'll never forget. That day I filed for bankruptcy and started my consulting firm.

I had been in the computer industry for 20 years, having started and operated several successful businesses. My most recent venture had been my new invention, the world's first electronic yellow pages! It was a great idea, yet when I brought in some outsiders in order to raise some badly needed capital, I lost control of my own company!

A period of political infighting left me on the outside of my own company. For the next year, I lived on credit cards in a state of depression. Then the personal bankruptcy took away my plastic.

Not too long afterward, I found myself sleeping on a used mattress in a studio apartment. I didn't have a car and had to borrow a friend's in order to make a sales call.

So what did I do? I became a consultant, just like a million other broke, unemployed guys. My office furniture was a wooden folding chair and a door laid across a couple of two-drawer files.

I had to find some clients *pronto!* But how could I, with no money to advertise and no car?

Without the financial resources, I knew that I had to come up with an idea to drum up some business that didn't require a bundle of cash.

In my empty wallet, I found a yellowed, tattered article that 10 years ago I had cut out of *The Wall Street Journal.* It listed 10 rules for entrepreneurs. Based on my personal experiences, I revised the list and christened it THE 10 COMMANDMENTS FOR MANAGING A YOUNG, GROWING BUSINESS. After several rewritings, I said to myself: "This is the kind of stuff I wish I had been taught a long time ago!"

Using credit, I convinced a local printer to print a total of 200 copies of the list on a 17" × 11" cardboard poster, with "Michael McCafferty & Associates" and my phone number on the bottom.

Next, I hired Marianne, a friend's girlfriend—a pretty girl with a lovely smile—to work for me on a commission basis. I promised to give her a percentage of my profits derived from anyone who became a client as a result of her work. Marianne was a full-time waitress who relied on tips, so working on commission for me suited her fine. Thank heavens. Because I didn't have the money to pay her up front.

I instructed her to stop at every business in a large industrial park in Sorrento Valley on the north side of San Diego. Her job was to give a poster to every businessperson in the area.

Knowing I had a computer background, Marianne said to me, "I know nothing about computers. What am I supposed to say to people?"

"Just one word," I coached her. *"Computers."*

"Computers? That's it?" she asked.

"And say it as if you are asking a question. You know, 'Computers?' I want you to have a question mark in your voice. Also, don't forget to give 'em your beautiful smile."

I wanted to keep it simple, realizing that there would be a problem if any business owners asked her questions since she knew nothing about computers.

"What do I do next?" Marianne questioned.

"Don't say a single word after you say, 'Computers?' Wait for them to reply. If somebody says, 'Yes,' point down at the bottom of the poster and say, 'Call this number if you have any questions,' and then turn around and leave."

"What if they say, 'No'?" she asked.

"Point to my name and phone number and say, 'Call this number if you have any questions.' Then get out. Don't say another word."

It took her about two days to pass out the 200 posters, and then the phone started to ring. A few people called only because they wanted another poster, but 25 genuine prospects also responded— enough to get me started in my consulting business. And Marianne received about $2000 in commissions for her two-day job. From that point on, I never had to go out and make cold calls for new clients. From the business my 10 commandments posters generated, and the referrals and repeat business that followed, it didn't take long before I was making a decent living as a computer consultant.

I primarily consulted with small business owners on computer programs and software that would serve their needs. Sean Curtis was one of the first people to receive a 10 commandments poster. A man in his mid-twenties, Sean had a couple of salespeople working for his small, growing company, which provided coffee service to offices and warehouses. I recommended a software program for his company that kept records on his customers, including such things as inventory and billing information. Six months later, Sean informed me that while the program had done wonders for his business, and his company expanded, there were some things the software couldn't handle.

I studied his needs and understood his problem. It wasn't the first time I'd come across the limitations of this program. You see, every software program has certain drawbacks. Many can't be integrated with other software. Some companies lacked good customer support. Others didn't have a network version. The list went on and on, and I realized nothing in the marketplace would do the complete job for Sean.

Why should I put my customers into these software programs, when none of the programs was doing a superior job? By the time Sean approached me, I had already said to myself, "If just one more customer comes to me with these requirements, I am going to do whatever it takes to get the job done for them—even if I have to write the software program myself."

After reviewing Sean's problems, I decided to design a software program that not only would fit Sean's needs, but would also work for other small business owners. Since I knew exactly what entrepreneurial clientele needed, by George, I'd be the one to design a program for them!

I said to Sean, "I want you to pay me to write this program for you. But I need to own it, so I can sell it to others too. If you agree to that, I'll give you free upgrades as I continually improve it. Okay?"

Sean gave me the go-ahead.

I worked on the program for about six months, and Sean ended up paying me $5000 in fees. As a direct result of the program, his business, Coffee Ambassador, started to expand by leaps and bounds, and Sean is the first to say that he got more than his money's worth out of it.

For me, it was the beginning of a new life. The software program, which I named TELEMAGIC, was the most practical, simple, user-friendly software program ever devised for its market. It was designed so that people without computer skills could easily learn it.

When TELEMAGIC was first introduced, I sold it through advertising in telemarketing magazines. The program retailed for $95. That was a revolutionary price when some telemarketing software sold for tens of thousand of dollars. At the time, personal computers were being introduced, which meant people could get into telemarketing for relatively little money.

Later I started distributing the program through dealers, and, believe it or not, I got complaints from them. "Your software is really terrific," they'd tell me. "The only problem is people don't believe it will do all it does for only $95. You have to raise your price."

"Look, if I charge more, you'd have to pay more."

"That's okay," they told me, "because we'll make more."

I thought to myself, "What a great business I'm in. People are telling me to raise my price!" I raised the price to $195, then to $295, $495, and later on, $695. We began selling network versions of the software which retailed for $795 and later sold for $1295, $1500, and $1995. We even sold TELEMAGIC corporate licenses to Fortune 500 corporations for sums in excess of $100,000 each.

All in all, we sold more than 200,000 TELEMAGIC programs. My business was booming. But it was killing me! It was eating me alive. In the beginning I enjoyed it, because I'm basically a creative person and can work comfortably in a company with 10 or so employees. But I am not good at the administrative end of a business. And as the business grew, I had to hire more people and pour more money into the company to keep it going. The company couldn't stand still. It had go either forward or backward.

It's like playing in a poker game in which you buy in with a nickel. Then you start winning thousands and it runs into millions, and you're playing for eight years. Every time you get a hand, you push the entire pot of millions back in. But you're winning only one nickel at a time. That's the way my business was. I felt as though I risked everything, every day I was in business. At the same time, my competitors were getting bigger and stronger, and more and more of them came at me. When I first started TELEMAGIC, I had no competitors; now there were more than 600 software programs that had come out in the marketplace. As the saying goes, "Success breeds competition."

I felt enormous pressure, and I was getting a pain in my side that just wouldn't go away. I finally went to a doctor, who said there was nothing wrong with me. *It was stress.*

In early 1992, I met with a business broker and instructed him to find a buyer for my business. "This business is killing me," I said. "I want out."

I had studied my business and hired an independent analyst to determine its worth. "I want $7 million for it," I told the broker, "all in cash."

"Maybe I can get you $7 million," he said, "but you may have to take some stock certificates instead of cash."

"No paper," I insisted. "Look, I've got paper now. I can sell this company only once, and if the stock goes down, I've just wasted eight years of my life." In view of my two past experiences of creating wealth only to lose it all, I wanted financial security that would last me a lifetime.

"We'll sell this business," he said, "but don't get discouraged if I don't get you your number."

"If I don't get the number, I don't sell," I said.

After talking to a dozen or so buyers, six actually came in to look my company over. One potential buyer was Sage Group, a British company headquartered in Newcastle-Upon-the-Tyne. Sage owned a U.S. subsidiary, DacEasy, the largest accounting software company in the world, and TELEMAGIC looked like a good fit. After several meetings, an offer was made, but not at the price and terms I wanted. Sage offered me $1 million less than what I was asking.

I met with them and said: "I can do this only one time, isn't that right? Now you're going to want me to stay around for a while and help you with the business. In order for me to be able to properly help your company, I must have the right spirit. To have the right spirit, I've got to know I made the right deal. Only when I know I got the right number for this company will I feel as though I owe you my best effort.

"Now from your point of view, it's just money—and you've got it," I continued. "What you really want is a company that will make you *a lot* of money. I'm the guy who'll make this $7 million investment pale in comparison with what you'll make over the next several years.

"Look at it this way: We're only $1 million apart from making a deal. For a company your size, this amount of money is irrelevant. Mark my words, this is going to be one of the smartest moves you ever made. It would be very unfortunate for you to walk away from it because you're $1 million short of my asking price."

Evidently my logic made good sense to them. In October 1992, Sage bought my company for $7 million, plus 15 percent of their sales for the next 27 months, which means what I was paid could potentially be worth a total of $13 million.

There are several good lessons in this story. First, Michael McCafferty, who was having dire financial problems, never gave up. Down for the nine-count, through sheer tenacity and ingenuity, he came up with a clever way to attract clients to use his consulting services. Incredibly, one of those first clients, Coffee Ambassador, had a special software need. McCafferty's programming became the catalyst for TELEMAGIC, a multi-million-dollar enterprise that made him a wealthy man. As McCafferty puts it, "When you go out and knock on doors, you never know what good fortune lies behind them." A second important lesson in this story is illustrated by McCafferty's determination to stick by his guns and hold out for the price and terms he believed his business was worth—and get it!

Michael McCafferty began his career in 1964 as an IBM sales rep. After a variety of successes in the computer industry, he formed Michael McCafferty & Associates, a one-man consulting firm, in 1983. His company evolved into TELEMAGIC, a firm that produced the number-one sales software program in the world.

THE BLIND DENTIST

Told by Jerry Heffel

As president of The Southwestern Company since 1980, I work with an organization of thousands of college students who spend their summers as independent contractors selling educational books directly to consumers. In fact, this is exactly how I worked my way through college in the early 1960s.

Southwestern's history dates way back to 1855, when it began as a small publishing company right here in Nashville, Tennessee. Later, when many Southern families were financially devastated by the Civil War, the company began a summer sales program to provide young men and women with a way to earn money for their college educations. We've been doing that ever since, and as a result, tens of thousands of Americans have gone to college, becoming doctors, attorneys, stockbrokers, entrepreneurs, bankers, judges, and so on.

With so many student salespeople going through our training program, I've witnessed many interesting stories, but my favorite concerns Jim Baker, a young predental student from the state of Washington.

In 1980, Jim had just finished his sixth summer with us, and at age 24, was our number-two salesperson in the nation out of a field of nearly 4000. That June, he had graduated from the University of Washington and was scheduled to enroll in the School of Dentistry at Ohio State University in the fall. Having worked very hard for three solid months selling books in Texas, Jim drove through Nashville on his way to Columbus, Ohio. In Nashville, he stopped by to pick up a check for approximately $20,000, which represented the profits he made for the summer.

Jim was obviously quite proud of his accomplishments. He had made President's Club in Sales Achievement for 12 out of 12 weeks. His top personal income week was $3600 in today's dollars, and he was a top sales team manager. Jim was so enthusiastic when he visited our headquarters, he was glowing. It was evident that he felt on top of the world when he walked through our offices, stopping to greet everyone along the way.

Jim, who had wanted to be a dentist since age 13, had a 4.0 grade point average in undergraduate school. He was excited to enter dental school, and continued to work for us during the summer months. In 1983, he headed the company's number-one student organization, and in a speech he made that year, Jim stated, "Learning to meet and work with people is great preparation for building a dental practice. I met with doctors, lawyers, farmers, unemployed people, teachers, businesspeople—such a wide range—and that's the sort of clientele you develop as a dentist. What I've learned was a heck of a lot more important than anything I could have learned as a volunteer in a dentist's office."

After graduating from dental college, Jim started a practice in Mansfield, Ohio. His practice was flourishing when, in April 1986, he began to have fluid buildup in the back of his eyes. Jim received laser surgery, but had complications which stemmed from taking insulin shots for diabetes for 15 years. Later, he was diagnosed as having diabetic retinopathy. By the end of the year, Jim was totally blind.

It was tragic. Jim studied for 10 years in undergraduate and dental school, took his licensing examinations, started his practice, and now within a year he was sightless.

As Jim puts it: "I went from seeing fine in April to six months later, seeing nothing. I had spent so much time in school, and I was enjoying my practice. Then I knew I would never be able to work in my chosen field.

"When my sight started going," he continues, "I knew what was happening, so I used that time to figure out what to do next. Selling books during all those summers taught me that when there is a problem, you do your best to solve it and move on. From my sales experiences I learned how important attitude is. I also realized there wasn't a darn thing I could do about my blindness. I was 30 years old, and if I just felt sorry for myself for the rest of my life, I was destined to have a very miserable life.

"So I thought, 'What can I do? What training do I have?' Dentistry wasn't an option. After all, a blind dentist? The only other marketable experience I had was my sales experience with Southwestern."

Jim went back to the state of Washington and contacted Dr. Carl Roberts in Nashville, Tennessee. Carl heads Southwestern's Professional Services division, a placement executive recruitment search firm originally formed to counsel our student salespeople so they could secure jobs when they're finished with school. The service is free to the students and funded entirely by placement fees paid by the hiring companies.

After several meetings with Jim, Carl called me. He pointed out Jim's impressive track record with Southwestern during his college days, and talked about his incredible attitude. "You know, Jerry," Carl said, "since our personnel placement business is conducted by phone, there is nothing to prevent someone with Jim's qualities from being a top producer."

To our good fortune, Jim accepted our offer to become part of our Nashville staff in 1987. Today, Dr. Jim Baker is a certified personnel consultant in Professional Services. He interviews and counsels young students who seek career guidance. Jim also contacts companies that want to recruit bright, aggressive young people.

Today, Jim's office is equipped with dictating machines, scanners that read information aloud, and computers that employ a voice simulator card to retrieve information stored in his client databases. A modest man, Jim credits much of his success to Laurie Lea (when he refers to AI), "my great secretary, who reads a lot of stuff to me."

One of Southwestern's top recruiters, Jim has lined his office walls with sales awards. Other awards have been presented to him at annual conventions of the Tennessee Association of Personnel Consultants.

"Jim is the consummate professional in this business," says his manager, Greg Boucher. "Of course, he's human; he goes through slumps and rides hot streaks like every salesperson. But Jim has never used his visual impairment as an excuse for falling short of a production goal."

When Jim Baker sold books to finance his dental education, nobody could have predicted it would lead to what he does today. But as it turned out, those sales experiences provided Jim with what has since become his life's work.

The lessons Jim Baker learned as a young book salesperson were invaluable to him as a mature man. He took what he learned those summers about dealing with rejection and overcoming obstacles and applied these lessons outside the sales arena to life itself. Who would have blamed Jim Baker had he thrown in the towel, claiming that life dealt him a bad hand? Instead, with the right mental attitude, he chose to live with a positive philosophy. He refused to allow himself to be defeated by the handicap of blindness.

Jerry Heffel has been associated with The Southwestern Company since 1965, when he began as a student salesperson during his college years. Since its beginning in 1855, Southwestern has provided tens of thousands of students with summer sales opportunities to (1) make money to apply to their college educations and (2) gain valuable experience in the process. Nearly a century and a half old, the company originally sold religious books, but today specializes in educational publications. Heffel has been president of Southwestern since 1980. He has also served as chairman of the Direct Selling Association in Washington, D.C., the national trade association for the industry, and as chairman of the Direct Selling Education Association.

IT'S NOT THE TERRITORY

Told by Robert L. Shook

In 1962, a year after my father and I started our insurance agency in Pittsburgh, I learned a wonderful lesson about mental attitude. It happened when one of our agents, who was given 20 sales leads in the Pittsburgh suburb of Penn Hills, complained about his territory.

In those days, to us a sales lead was the name of a business owner, with address and occupation typed on a note card. In reality, it was a cold call—the only difference was that the agent knew who to ask for after walking through the door. Our sales approach was simply to walk into a business establishment, look at the note card, and say in a very important manner: "I'm looking for Mr. Smith."

"I'm Mr. Smith," the owner would say.

"Mr. Smith, my name is Robert Shook, and I have some very important information to discuss with you concerning your self-employment."

Not knowing I was selling long-term disability insurance, the prospect would typically reply, "What about?"

"I said it was important," I'd firmly state. "May we talk in private? What I have to say is highly confidential."

Not knowing whether I might represent the IRS or the FBI, the owner would rarely ask questions. Instead, we'd go into the prospect's office and I'd start my sales presentation.

It took about five minutes before the prospect realized I was selling a long-term disability policy. The prospect would listen out of either politeness or aroused interest. After all, our sales presentation emphasized to the prospect: "Your earnings are dependent upon your ability to get out of bed each day and go to work. In the event you are sick or injured with a long-term disability, your business and your savings will eventually be wiped out." It was a highly emotional sales pitch; we believed health insurance was most effectively sold by appealing to one's emotions.

A brochure outlining the benefits of the policy was used throughout the sales presentation. My father and I had designed the brochure, and at the time, we felt it was the most convincing piece of sales literature in our industry.

Well, at one particular Saturday meeting, Bill Fox (a fictitious name) was down in the dumps and announced: "I called on 20 prospects and was unable to make a single sale. These leads that were given to me are worthless. The Penn Hills area is no good and I insist on having a different territory."

Herb Shook, my father, who was conducting the sales meeting, did not appreciate Fox's negative remarks, especially in the presence of our entire nine-agent sales force. Three trainees were present, and it wasn't in their best interest to believe that one territory was better than another.

"Perhaps it's not the territory but your mental attitude that needs changing," Herb suggested.

"I'm telling you, nobody could have sold these prospects," Fox insisted.

"Is that so?" replied my father. A man who loved a good challenge, he continued: "I'll tell you what I'll do. To prove it's not the territory that's no good but the salesman, I will take these same 20 leads and sell a minimum of 10 of them next week! If I don't, after next week's meeting I'll treat everyone to a steak lunch while I eat beans. But if I succeed, every one of you will eat beans for lunch, while I enjoy a nice steak!"

Everyone, including Fox, agreed to the steak-or-beans lunch.

"What in the world is he doing?" I thought to myself. "How will he ever get those same 20 businesspeople to listen to the identical sales presentation they heard a week before? Not only will he waste his time, he'll shake the confidence of our sales force by not being able to make his self-imposed sales quota."

"Karen," my father shouted to our secretary in the next room. "Please make copies of these 20 lead cards and pin them on the bulletin board." Then, turning to our small group, he said, "You guys will see that the applications and premium checks I'll bring in next Saturday will match the same lead cards."

I had to admit I was impressed with how my father was able to inspire our sales force by pledging to do the "impossible." He certainly generated an excitement in the room for the remainder of the sales meeting. "But what will their mood be next week when he fails to deliver?" I asked myself.

After the meeting, I said to him, "I think you bit off more than you can chew, and what you did will end up hurting morale."

"We'll see next week, son," he said.

For the next five days, Herb called on the same 20 prospects Fox had visited the previous week. Throughout the week, he refused to reveal to me or anyone else his results. Whenever asked, he'd say, "I'll give my full report next Saturday morning."

Finally Saturday morning arrived, and everyone was anxious to find out who would be eating beans and who would be eating steak for lunch.

At the meeting, Herb opened his briefcase in front of everyone and pulled out a single application. Attached to it was a check. "This one is Fred Williams."

"He's the owner of the hardware store," a surprised Bill Fox responded.

Then Herb took out a second application from his briefcase and read a second name. To add a spice of melodrama to the sales meeting, he repeated the process until 16 signed applications were stacked on the conference table. Only four of the prospects that Fox had called on the previous week didn't buy. We gave him a long standing ovation.

"How did you do it?" Fox asked in astonishment.

"When I called on each of the 20 prospects, I introduced myself by saying, 'I'm Herb Shook with Fidelity Interstate (the insurance company our agency represented). I understand Bill Fox was here to see you last week,'" Herb explained.

"'Well, I am here again because the company just came out with a brand new policy, and it offers considerably more benefits than the old one offered to you last week and at the same cost. Now this will just take a minute to show you the differences.' Before anyone could say no, I pulled out the identical brochure Bill showed them and I reviewed it again, using the exact sales presentation—word for word—as Bill, but each time I really poured on the enthusiasm. I'd emphasize, 'Now listen very carefully to this feature because it's brand new.' Then I'd add, 'Now do you see the difference?' and each time they'd say, 'Boy, that is different!'

"'Now listen to this,' I'd continue, 'I really think this new feature is exceptional,' and I'd explain another benefit. 'Now what do you think about that?' I'd ask, and again, the response was, 'That is different!' Then I'd go on and say, 'Now I want you to pay especially close attention to this next feature, because everybody is really excited about it.' I kept selling with all the enthusiasm I could muster. By the time I was through with each sales presentation, everyone was as enthusiastic as I. Every one of them thanked me for calling on them to show them the new policy—even the four who didn't buy."

Shortly afterward, Herb grinned. "I can hardly wait for lunch because I'm in the mood for a juicy, medium-rare steak! And I hope you all enjoy your beans."

As my father used to say, "Nothing is as contagious as enthusiasm." It was not an original quote, but until the lesson he taught us that Saturday morning, I never knew its true meaning. Another thing he stressed was: "It is not only what a salesperson says, but how he or she says it that counts."

I also learned it's not the territory that counts; it's the salesperson who makes the difference. Never afterward did I blame the territory when my sales were down.

This incident occurred during our first year in business. Over the years, our agency expanded and grew into a dynamic sales organization with more than 200 full-time agents representing us in 22 states. Eleven years later, we formed our own life insurance company, American Executive Life Insurance Company. My father served as its president and I as chairman of the board. To a large measure, our company's growth was a direct result of my father's enthusiasm.

THE INITIAL APPROACH

Anyone who has ever sold anything knows that getting his or her foot in the door is a prerequisite for making a sale. After all, to use a baseball analogy, you can't get a hit if you never get up to bat.

There is a vast army of salespeople out there knocking on doors and soliciting via the telephone, so it is no wonder a majority of prospects have an initial resistance to salespeople. Sometimes, it is not the actual prospect who offers the first resistance, but instead a person whom I refer to as the "gatekeeper." This is an individual who has the job of screening out salespeople—and allows only a handful to see the boss! Generally, the gatekeeper is a receptionist, a secretary, or an assistant.

Of course, any salesperson worth his or her salt makes sure to be one of the chosen few who gets past the gatekeeper. As you read this part, you'll witness that getting through to see the prospect has little to do with what company you represent or, for that matter, even with what you sell. Instead, it depends on your ability to make the right first impression!

YOU MEET THE NICEST INVESTORS ON THE GOLF COURSE

Told by Alan "Ace" Greenberg

O ne of the men in this industry whom I greatly admired was Salim "Cy" Lewis. A fabulous salesman, Cy was Bear Stearns' senior partner, assuming the leadership of the firm back in 1936. In 1956, two years before I became a partner of the firm, I worked on the trading floor at a desk next to Lewis, and I got to know him very well. Cy is the man acclaimed for being the "inventor" of block trading. He started the bidding of blocks of stock much the same way people had been bidding on bonds. He did this with certain institutional accounts, and I credit him for putting Bear Stearns on the map.

I joined Bear Stearns in 1949, and I still remember hearing how Cy would say he'd like to have Robert R. Young as a client. Back then, Young was one of the nation's most prominent business leaders. A self-made man from Canadian, a small rural town in northwest Texas, Young acquired control and served as chairman of Alleghany Corp. Later he bought interests in 23,000 miles of railroads in the United States, including the Chesapeake & Ohio Railway Co., another company of which he served as chairman of the board from 1942 until 1954. After resigning as C&O's chairman in 1954, Young led a famous proxy fight that got control of the New York Central Railroad and then served as its board chairman. So you can see, Robert Young was one of the major players back in the 1940s and 1950s. No wonder Cy Lewis wanted very much to have Young as a client.

Young was a very social man, and Lewis was not, so as much as he tried, Lewis was unable to get an introduction to meet him. Yet Lewis was determined to do business with him. One day, Cy found out that Young, an avid golfer, played golf every spring at the Greenbrier, the world-renowned resort in White Sulphur Springs, West Virginia. That's when Cy came up with a great idea on how to meet Young.

Cy called the Greenbrier and said, "I would like to come down for 10 days, and during my stay, I would like to engage the golf pro for the entire time I am a guest."

Naturally, the golf pro was delighted to accommodate him, and Cy booked the pro solidly for the 10-day period. After a few days of playing with the pro, the pro said to Cy, "Mr. Lewis, I am sorry but I won't be able to play with you tomorrow."

"What do you mean?" Cy asked.

"Well, another person is coming down whom I have to play with."

"We have a deal," Cy said. "You have to play with me every day. However, if this guy wants to join us, that's fine with me."

The pro agreed, and of course the other guy was Robert Young.

For the rest of the vacation, the two of them played golf together, and by the end of the week a wonderful friendship had bloomed.

As a consequence, Cy did an incredible amount of business with Young. For instance, Cy sold him control of Investors Diversified Services (IDS). Cy bought it at a price and gave Young an option for 24 hours to buy at a higher price. That's how Alleghany Corp. became the owner of IDS, which it later sold to American Express.

"Ace" Greenberg, who, today, is one of the most admired and highly respected members of the investment community, has told this story several times to his associates at Bear Stearns. The story illustrates how a salesperson can be innovative and aggressive in meeting a very important prospect. While unconventional, Cy Lewis's approach got the job done, and it resulted in millions of dollars of business.

Alan "Ace" Greenberg was named CEO of Bear Stearns in April 1978, a few days after Cy Lewis passed away. Although Greenberg heads one of the nation's most prestigious investment banking firms, he is still an active trader for his personal clients.

TAKING
THE *BULLY*
BY THE HORNS

Told by Robert L. Shook

When I was in my early 20s, I sold life insurance. On trips between Columbus and other Ohio cities, I would frequently drive the old state highways—on prospecting missions. I observed that the owners of big farms were particularly good prospects, and an especially good time of day to call on them was at the noon hour. During the summer months, when the sun was the hottest, they'd take a dinner break. (A city boy, it took me a while to learn that lunch was "dinner" and the evening meal was "supper.")

One blistering hot summer day, I drove by a magnificent farm. The land was rolling, the silo and barn buildings were in tip-top shape, and the large farmhouse was freshly painted. Yessir, this looked like a wonderful prospect. I looked at my watch and it was ten minutes after twelve. I spotted the farmer on his tractor in the middle of a large field of wheat. It was time for him to take a break and get out of the hot sun—and it was dinner time! I parked my car on the side of the country road, noted the farmer's name from the mailbox, and walked part way through the field in his direction.

"Hey, Mr. Jenkins," I yelled as loud as I could so he could hear me over the roar of the tractor. "Come on over here."

"What for?" he yelled back.

"I have some important information to tell you," I shouted. "You are William Jenkins, aren't you?"

He drove across the field, parked his tractor, turned off his engine, climbed down, and started walking to me. As he did, it was as if the ground was starting to shake. He was six feet five inches and must have weighed 250 pounds.

"Important? It better be important!" he growled.

After I identified myself, I could see his face turn a slow beet red. "I swore I'd take the next son-of-a-gun who tried to sell me insurance," he bellowed, "and throw him bodily off my land."

I looked at him straight in the eye and said, "Let me tell you something, my friend. Before you try anything like that with me, you better take out all the insurance you can get because you're going to need it."

There was a moment of silence, and I didn't bat an eyelash. Neither did he. Then he burst out laughing. "What the hell. On a hot day like this, I could use a break. Come on over to the house and let's hear what you've got." He put his arm around my shoulder and we headed toward his house.

We walked into his kitchen, and he said to his wife, "Hey, honey, I want you to meet Bob Shook. Do you want to hear a good one? This young man thinks he could take me." With that, they both laughed so hard, I thought they were going to burst. I broke out into laughter too. When the laughing stopped, I made one of the easiest sales I ever had.

Mr. Jenkins wasn't the first person to threaten me when I identified myself as an insurance agent, although he might have been the biggest. From my past experiences, I learned never to back off when a prospect roared at me in a threatening manner. I understood, "Nobody is really going to physically hit a salesperson, no matter how upset and angry he or she might be." As a young man, I figured the odds of that happening were so astronomically high that they were literally off the charts. And even if somebody did take a swing at me, I could live with it. With this thinking, I became fearless. I approached all prospects with complete confidence and they could sense it. Consequently, it was a rare occasion when I would encounter any resistance when making a cold call—even to sell insurance!

THE GOLF BUDDIES

Told by Richard Connolly

I don't solicit business from friends and relatives. I know that many stockbrokers do, and I'm not saying they shouldn't. It's just a personal thing with me—I don't want people to think I used my relationship with them to make a sale. Besides, when I'm away from my office, I don't like mixing business with pleasure.

This is particularly true when I play golf, one of my favorite recreations. I've loved the game ever since I was a kid and caddied at a local country club. Growing up, I dreamed about someday being on the PGA tour. In college, I was captain of the Holy Cross golf team.

So now you know where I come from when I tell you I have a cardinal rule never to do business on the golf course. Understand, some of the best prospects I come in contact with are indeed members of my country club. Nonetheless, I try to separate my private life from my business life.

I don't mean to say that none of my golf buddies are clients. It's just that I never aggressively solicited them for business. On the other hand, when they approach me, I don't turn them down.

For instance, in one summer of 1980, I was matched with Larry Ansin in a foursome at the club. We enjoyed a good round of golf, and over a period of time, Larry and I began playing together regularly. Our games were fairly evenly matched, and being the same age, we shared similar interests, particularly in sports. In time, a warm friendship blossomed.

Larry was CEO of Joan Fabrics, a large, privately owned supplier of upholstery used mainly in the automobile and furniture industries. His company was second only to Wang Industries as the biggest employer in the city of Lowell, Massachusetts.

Obviously Larry was a prime prospect for me. Still, I never suggested he use me as his stockbroker. It's just not my style.

He did know I was with PaineWebber. After all, I don't keep what I do for a living a secret. Since Larry was a successful businessperson, it wasn't unusual for the two of us to talk business. He would ask me questions about a company or an industry; sometimes, he'd seek my opinion on the stock market in general. Although I was never shy about answering, not once did I show an inclination to open an account for him.

Every now and then, Larry would request that I get him a report. Or he'd ask, "Can you check this out for me with an analyst at PaineWebber?" I was happy to oblige, still never suggesting we do business together.

One day, out of the clear blue sky, Larry put his arm on my shoulder and said, "Dick, you've been doing a lot for me, and I know you are successful at what you do. But you have never solicited me for my business."

"That's right, Larry, I haven't."

"So, Dick, let me tell you what I'm getting at," he said in his soft manner. "I want to open an account with you."

I smiled and let him continue.

"As far as I am concerned, Dick, you have excellent credibility. I respect the fact that you have never solicited me, because I am basically the same way. I don't like to get involved in business transactions with friends either. Now that I've said that, my friend, I want to use you as my stockbroker."

The following Monday morning, he called me at the office and opened an account. In time, Larry became one of my largest accounts. He also referred me to several family members and business associates who also became clients.

Now would I have been able to open an account with Larry if I had aggressively approached him for his business? Perhaps, but I wouldn't have felt comfortable doing it—not with a good friend. However, I can assure you I am assertive in soliciting potential clients in other scenarios.

Unfortunately, this story ends on a sad note. In June 1993 my wife, Anne Marie, and I were on a PaineWebber trip in London when I received a call that Larry had succumbed to a brain tumor. We were devastated and came home immediately for his funeral. Larry had become one of my dearest friends, and I remember him as one of the nicest, brightest, most charitable people I have ever known.

As with most things in life, timing is everything. A professional salesperson knows when to come on strong and when to back off. Dick Connolly, one of the top producers in the securities industry, understands people and knows when to "soft sell." In particular, he doesn't feel comfortable soliciting friends at social gatherings. (This includes not only the golf course but dinner parties and other settings.) Affluent and influential people are especially on their guard because, as prime prospects, they are constantly being approached by salespeople. To paraphrase F. Scott Fitzgerald, "The rich are different from other people." To them, a hard sell can become a real turnoff! As Connolly illustrates, long-term relationships develop and grow when nurtured over a period of time.

Richard F. Connolly, Jr., resides in Boston, Massachusetts, and is the number-one stockbroker for PaineWebber, Inc. He is ranked as one of the top 10 individuals in the securities field.

BEING THERE

Told by Betsy Martin

In 1982, one year after joining *Money* magazine as a sales rep, I was transferred to Boston, where I became the company's first salesperson in New England. During my first week on the job, it was a little past 6 p.m. and I was getting ready to leave the office when the telephone rang. It was Mark Franklin, the advertising agency management supervisor for my largest account, Fidelity Investments, a major mutual fund company.

Franklin was upset over a discrepancy in his invoice. Before I could get a word in, he began to read the riot act to me.

"I'm sorry, sir, but I don't have any of the details," I replied. "Please let me check into this and get back with you tomorrow."

But no matter how reasonable I tried to be, he simply would not stop. He ranted and raved, refusing to let up.

Since Fidelity was my biggest account, I wanted to avoid confrontation. However, I drew the line when he began to swear at me.

"If you are going to shout," I told him, "you will force me to hang up. If you continue to use that language, we cannot talk."

This statement was intended to calm him down, or at the very least break the ice. Unfortunately, it had no such effect!

Finally I told him, "If you're going to yell at me, at least have the decency to do it to my face. You're only a couple of blocks away. Why don't I come over and we can talk about it?"

"Forget it! I'm too busy! I can't be bothered with this!" he snapped back. "Now, damn it, just take care of it!"

Before I could say a word, I was hearing a dial tone.

I couldn't get this conversation off my mind, which cause me to have a sleepless night. The next morning when I went back to the office, I called New York to have the accounting people pull the Fidelity file for me. I carefully reviewed it, tossed a copy in my briefcase, and headed straight for Franklin's office. I felt armed with all the ammunition I needed. Now all I had to do was get through to Franklin and give him an explanation. Surely seeing him face to face would nip the problem in the bud. Although he had been gruff over the phone, I didn't anticipate the same kind of treatment in person. After all, a man in his position rarely behaves uncivilly, particularly to a woman like me, who looks like a decent human being. Yes, seeing him in person should do the trick.

Fortunately, he happened to walk by as I was talking to the receptionist on his floor. "Oh, there's Mr. Franklin now," she said.

I mustered my nerve and caught up with him. "Mr. Franklin, I'm Betsy Martin from *Money.*" He stopped walking and, caught off guard, he seemed much meeker and milder.

"M-m—money?" he stammered. "Haven't we…"

"That's right, sir," I said as cheerfully as I could. "I have your file here in my briefcase so we can review it."

"I'm on my way to a…"

"Now that we've met face to face, maybe we can go over all these troubles you've been having with those billing discrepancies," I interrupted. "If I caught you at a bad time, I'll just sit down here in the lobby until you have time to see me so we can iron this out."

"Ms. Martin," he said apologetically, "won't you please come into my office? I am sure we can get this matter resolved in an amicable manner." We walked into his office, and he held the door open like a perfect gentleman!

Of course, we did get along well. Our meeting was the beginning of a wonderful long-term relationship. In time, we became good friends and continued to do the best work for our mutual client, Fidelity.

There are some business matters that must be transacted in person. A good salesperson recognizes these situations, and, in particular, when confrontation occurs, he or she meets it head on. Never, absolutely never, back away from a disgruntled customer. Instead, take the bull by the horns and directly tackle the problem. Remember that customer problems rarely go away by themselves. Intuitively, Martin knew she would be better received visiting in person, rather than remaining a faceless sales rep on the telephone. She was correct.

Betsy Martin is a publisher with Money. *In this capacity, she heads up the magazine's sales force, promotion, and public relations. She began her career with* Money *in 1981 as a sales representative in New York City.*

NEVER PREJUDGE

Told by Ebby Halliday

Early in my real estate career I learned that a salesperson should never prejudge a prospect. Back in the 1950s I was selling homes for Hal Anderson, a Dallas builder who was developing Mayflower Estates. He was doing something that had never been done before, building $100,000 homes on speculation—that is, without a specific buyer.

These luxury homes were equivalent to those presently in the $700,000 to $800,000 price range. Back then, no one risked large sums for a development of top-of-the-line homes unless they were presold. The venture was so unusual that *The Wall Street Journal* did a feature article on Mayflower Estates.

One day when I was holding an open house, Hal stopped by to say hello. Shortly afterward, a beat-up car pulled into the driveway, and an elderly, unkempt couple walked up to the front door. While I was greeting them with a warm hello, I caught a glimpse of Hal out of the corner of my eye. He was shaking his head and making a face that clearly signaled, "Don't waste your time with them."

It wasn't my nature to be impolite to anyone, so I warmly greeted them and extended the same courtesy I would to any prospective buyer. Convinced that I was wasting my time, Hal left in a huff. Since the house was empty and the builder had left, I figured I wouldn't be imposing on anyone, so why not show them the house!

As I took them through the home, they looked in awe at its ornate amenities. The 12-foot ceilings overwhelmed them. It was evident that they had never been in such a fine home, and I enjoyed having the privilege of showing it to such appreciative people.

After looking at the fourth bathroom, the husband sighed to his wife, "Imagine a house with four bathrooms." He then turned to me and said, "For years, we've dreamed about owning a house with more than a single bathroom."

She looked at her husband with tears in her eyes, and I noticed she gently squeezed his hand.

After they had seen every corner of the house, we ended up back in the living room. "Would it be all right if we talked in private for a few minutes?" he politely asked.

"Of course," I replied, and walked into the kitchen to leave them by themselves.

Five minutes later, she called out to me, "It's okay, you can come in now."

I walked into the living room, and he asked, "Miss Halliday, did you say it cost $100,000?"

"Yes," I answered.

A faint smile appeared on his face. He reached into his coat pocket and pulled out a worn envelope. He sat down on the stair and began to pull money out of the envelope, counting it until $100,000 in cash was stacked in neat piles on the steps. Now remember, this happened back in the days when there was no drug money! As it turned out, he was maitre d' at one of the leading Dallas hotel restaurants, and for years and years, they had lived frugally to save his tips.

Shortly after they left, Hal came back, and I showed him the signed contract. I handed him the envelope, and when he peeked in, I thought he was going to faint!

Never prejudge anyone. Seasoned salespeople tell countless stories proving that the adage "Never judge a book by its cover" pertains especially to the sales field.

Ebby Halliday is founder of Ebby Halliday Realtors, a firm with 900 agents and 19 offices in the Dallas area. In 1993, its sales volume exceeded $1.25 billion. It is the nation's largest privately owned residential real estate company.

A CAPTIVE AUDIENCE

Told by Neil Balter

On my way out of town, I hurried into a taxi in front of my apartment building at 64th Street and First Avenue in Manhattan. "Kennedy Airport," I instructed the driver.

When I was settled comfortably in the back seat, an unusually friendly New York cab driver started a conversation with me.

"Nice apartment building you live in," he said.

"Yes," I replied.

"Live there very long?"

"No," I answered.

"I bet you must have a really small closet there," he said."

This time he had my attention. "Oh, yeah," I said, "quite small."

"Have you ever heard of closet organizers?" he asked.

"Yes, I guess I have seen an ad or something mentioned in the newspapers about it."

"Really what I do is drive cabs part time, and full time I organize people's closets. What I actually do is I come in and put shelves and drawers and this and that in closets."

"Is that interesting work?" I inquired.

"Would you ever think about having that done?" he asked.

"Well, I don't know," I said. "I do need some extra closet space. Isn't there another closet company out there, California something?"

"You mean California Closet Company. They're the really big company in the business. I can do exactly what they can do but I can do it for less money."

"Oh, really?"

"Yeah," he said.

"Explain to me what you do."

With this, the driver gave me a detailed explanation about what a professional closet organizer does. When the cabbie finished, he added, "When you call up California Closet, and they come to your house to make an estimate, this is what you should do. Ask them to leave you a copy of the plans. Now they won't want to leave you anything, but if you tell them you need it to show your girlfriend or wife, they'll give you a copy. Then you call me and I'll do the same thing but for 30 percent less money."

"That sounds very interesting," I said. "Here, let me give you my business card, and if you call me at my office, we'll set up a meeting."

I handed him my card, and after he looked at it, he nearly had a heart attack. In fact, he nearly swerved off the road.

"Oh, my God," he shouted. "You're Neil Balter! You're the founder of California Closet. I saw you on the *Oprah Winfrey Show*, and I thought you had such a good idea, I went into the business myself."

He looked through the rear-view mirror and started to study me. "I should have recognized you. Gosh, Mr. Balter, I apologize. I didn't mean you guys were an expensive company. I didn't mean…"

"Calm down," I said, "I like your style. You're a pretty smart fellow and you're aggressive. I admire that. You have a captive audience in your cab, and you took advantage of it. It takes chutzpah to do what you do. Why don't you call me, and we'll see what we can do about having you become one of our salesmen?"

He came to work for us, and became one of California Closet's top salespeople.

In some types of sales positions, you never know who a potential customer might be. This is obviously true for a taxi driver. Before a passenger steps into a cab, the driver has no previous knowledge of the individual. In this particular case, the cab driver knew only that Balter lived in a nice apartment building. Of course, it was safe for him to assume that everybody has a shortage of closet space in New York City! Nonetheless, the cab driver/closet organizer took advantage of the opportunity to pitch to his captive audience. Less aggressive salespeople miss the opportunity to make a sales presentation. The cab driver knew how to make things happen. Too often, salespeople sit and wait for a prospect to make the first move.

Neil Balter is the former CEO of California Closet Company, which he founded in 1978 at the age of 18. When Balter began his company, it was also the beginning of a new industry! In 1990 California Closet was acquired by William Sonoma Company.

THE NEW KID ON THE BLOCK

Told by Edward Lubin

E arly in my career, I sold broadcast time for a television station in Cleveland, Ohio. As the rookie sales rep on the force, I was handed the worst accounts—a station tradition. These were prospects who had been previously called on and never bought any time. Or worse, they were previous accounts that stopped buying from the station as a result of a particular problem.

So when my sales manager handed me several dozen 3" × 5" cards and said, "Go get 'em, kid," I knew he wasn't doing me any favor. In retrospect, it was a dumb thing to do to a novice sales-man. It's not exactly how you build confidence in someone. But the boss said, "Go get 'em, Lubin," and that's what I attempted to do. I made the rounds to prospects whose cards I had, and one by one, I got shot down. It was depressing, and I was ready to hang it up and tell my boss, "This is ridiculous. Why can't I get some good new accounts to call on?" But something inside kept me from telling him that. I suppose it was a matter of pride. Just the same, the constant rejection was getting to me and I was really feeling down.

Several days went by and I still had not made my first sale. Then at an early-morning sales meeting, the sales manager announced to the staff that the 11 p.m. weather slot was open for sale. The idea hit me that this is a very prestigious strip for television time and many customers want to buy it locally. "That's what I'll concentrate on," I thought to myself. "I'll sell the 11 p.m. slot."

Upon leaving the meeting, I carefully studied my lead cards and I came across a former customer who manufactured pasta on the west side of town. The card was well marked. It indicated that he had not bought from our station for five years, and notes were written on it by several other sales reps who had since called on him. The first note said, "He hates our station." Another one read, "Refuses to talk to station reps on the phone." And a third one stated, "This man is a nut case! Stay away! *Violent!*"

The comments of the other reps actually made me laugh. "How bad can this guy be?" I thought to myself. "And what a coup it would be if I came in with his name on an order pad. Man, I've got to sell this guy."

His plant was on the far side of town, so it took me half an hour to get there. All the way out, I kept pumping myself up with the thought: "He bought from us before, so I can get him to do it again." I kept repeating out loud, "I know I am going to sell him. I know it, I know it, I know it." Then, when I got to his building, I pulled right in front and suddenly it hit me, "But what if I don't sell him?" I took the card out again and stared at it for 10 minutes. Soon I was thinking, "He's probably worse than I can even imagine. What am I even doing here? I'm not going in there."

Then the thought struck me, "I didn't drive all the way over here just to be afraid to get out of my car. Don't be a coward, Lubin, go on in. There's not much he can do except throw you out. And what are odds that he'll do that? What have I got to lose?"

Finally, I got myself psyched up, got out of the car, and walked up the front sidewalk toward the building's main entrance. I looked inside, and the place was dark. I rang a buzzer beside the door; still, nobody came. "Good," I heard myself thinking. "I don't have to go through this after all." Then suddenly, I saw this really big person walking down the dark hall toward me. I knew it was the owner because one of the descriptions on the card referred to him as an overgrown Neanderthal man. He was an imposing figure with a mean look about him.

My first reaction was to turn around and head back to my car, but it was too late. He was bending down to unlock the revolving door.

He was dressed in a pair of jeans and a T-shirt, and there I was in my Brooks Brothers suit. "Hi," my voice managed to squeak out, "I'm Ed Lubin with WJW-TV."

"Get the hell out of here," he shouted. He looked very angry and the veins in his neck were starting to enlarge.

I was all set to accommodate him, but instead I found myself saying, "No, wait a minute. I'm the new kid on the block. I want you to give me five minutes to hear me out."

He pushed open the door and started to walk down the hall, motioning to me to follow him. I followed him to his office.

He sat behind his desk and literally began to growl at me. He told me a long story about how badly my station had handled his account. He told me that the other salespeople let him down because they never did anything they promised.

"Look at this card," I said to him. "Here's what they say about you."

He stared at it and didn't say a word.

Neither one of us said anything, and then I broke the ice. "Look, it doesn't matter what happened before. That's water over the dam. And it doesn't matter what you think about them or what they think about you. What does matter is that the 11 p.m. weather slot is open—that's a prime slot and it will be good for your business to get on it. Let's do that and I promise you I will take care of you like never before. I won't let you down."

"That's enough," he said. "How much is it?"

I quoted him the price and he replied, "Okay, Lubin, you got a deal."

When I got back to the station and showed the order to the other sales reps, I felt as though I was 10 feet tall. Never again did I hesitate to call on the so-called tough prospect.

Don't build up in your mind that a prospect will be difficult to approach. Sometimes the ones who are supposedly the most hard to get through to are not so difficult after all. Besides, you have nothing to lose by calling on them. And once you do sell them, it's a tremendous boost to your confidence when you call on other prospects. In comparison, everyone else will seem like a piece of cake!

Ed Lubin is a Pittsburgh transplant who now lives in the Los Angeles area, where he is in radio and television syndication and still calling on "the hard ones."

KEEPING
IN TOUCH

Told by Terrie Williams

W hile I was working as vice president and director of corporate communications at *Essence* magazine, I had what I considered my "dream" job. As the black woman's number-one lifestyle magazine, *Essence* was the place to be.

I had been with the magazine for nearly five years. Even though I was very happy with my career, I always knew that someday I would have my own company. I didn't know where or how it would unfold, but I felt it was only a matter of time before I'd run my own public relations firm. I had no reason to feel this way! After all, I had no agency experience, and I knew nothing about running a business! I just knew I had impeccable instincts, and I felt I was a very good public relations practitioner at *Essence*.

It's interesting how one thing leads to another. In the early 1980s I met the renowned entertainer Miles Davis, never knowing what effect that chance meeting would have on my life. At the time, I was practicing social work at New York Hospital, and Miles was a hip surgery patient. I was always intrigued by him, so when word got out that he had been admitted, I stopped in his room to introduce myself. I visited every day, and by the time he checked out, we had become good friends.

We kept in touch, and one day in 1984 I received an invitation from his wife, Cicely Tyson, to be a guest at Miles's sixtieth birthday party. Only his close friends were invited, so being included was a real high for me. The party was to be held on a yacht in Marina Del Ray, just south of Los Angeles.

One of the guests was Eddie Murphy, and we were briefly introduced. There wasn't much conversation—just a quick "Hello" and "Glad to meet you."

I also met Kenneth Frith and Eddie's cousin, Ray Murphy, Jr., who both worked with Eddie. I enjoyed talking to them. When the yacht docked and the party ended, one of them said, "Terrie, Eddie's performing at the Comedy Club tonight. Would you like to come as our guest?"

"Sounds great," I replied.

Eddie put on a terrific performance, and after the show, I joined Kenneth and Ray for a round of drinks. Evidently Eddie had other plans because I didn't see him again that evening.

Now when I returned to New York, I could have simply chalked it up as a wonderful party and an interesting night at the Comedy Club with two great guys. But I chose not to. Instead, I decided not to let my new friendships die, and I continued to keep in touch with Kenneth and Ray. When I got back to my desk, I sent them letters expressing my appreciation for the hospitality they extended during my visit to the West Coast. I also put them on a complimentary subscription list at the magazine. Neither of these gestures was a big deal—it was just my way of expressing appreciation.

Incidentally, I used to subscribe to about 100 magazines and a dozen or so newspapers, and I would read just about everything I could get my hands on. Whenever someone would mention that he or she had an interest in a specific area, I'd log it in my mental computer. Then, every time I'd read something that I thought might interest one of these people, I'd send the article along with a personal note. I did this routinely, although I had no concrete idea what purpose it was going to serve. I just felt that sooner or later...

I had Eddie Murphy's home address and telephone number, so naturally every time I read an article that I thought would be of interest to Eddie and the guys, I sent it. These writings pertained to show business—music, films, television—anything I came across. This was my way of staying in touch and keeping my name in front of them.

After nearly two years of this, I slowly developed a rapport with Eddie Murphy and his people. Kenneth invited me to a few parties, where I became acquainted with Eddie Murphy's inner circle.

Once I was invited to the filming of *Raw,* Eddie's first concert. The movie was a huge success, and Eddie was catapulted to the number-one box office draw in the entire world.

Shortly afterward, I attended a screening of *Moonstruck,* and it turned out that the guy I invited to escort me was the only person of color present besides me. A woman approached me to introduce herself, and my first reaction was that she did so because she wanted to know why I was there. As it turned out, we had spoken to each other once before on the telephone. During this chance meeting she said, "I hear Eddie is looking for a PR person."

As soon as the words passed her lips, *I knew I was going to represent him.* Admittedly, I didn't know how I was going to pull it off. But just the same, I knew I would. In hindsight, it was quite an ambitious goal. Here I was wanting to start a public relations agency with the world's number-one box office draw as my very first client!

The first thing I did was put together as much information as I could about my background, referring to people who could vouch for my standard of work and ability to deliver. In my cover letter to Eddie, I explained, "We have been in each other's company off and on over the years, but you've probably never had a chance to know what it is I do or how I do it." I briefly mentioned what my job entailed, and I listed people in business, politics, and entertainment whom I had met during my years at *Essence*—people I felt would recommend me. I stated very clearly that I wanted to represent him as his public relations adviser. Once I "packaged" myself, I knew I'd still have to convince Eddie that I was the best person to do the job for him.

A month went by, and he did not respond to my letter. So I decided to call his home.

Ray Murphy answered the telephone, and as always, greeted me warmly. "Hey, Terrie," he said.

We chatted for a while, and Ray said, "Eddie is here now, and he would like to talk to you."

Eddie's unmistakable voice came on the line. "Terrie, I got your package, and I would love to have you represent me."

It was an unbelievable moment. With no idea how I was going to pull it off, frankly, I was scared. But deep inside I felt destined to have my own business. Now suddenly I had the opportunity to represent Eddie Murphy as my very first client. To me, this was a very clear sign about what I was supposed to do.

It sometimes takes months or even years before a door opens and a major sale is made. Terrie Williams demonstrates how a long-term relationship can be established with a prospective client even *before* the sale is made. This is also a story about persistence. Terrie invested considerable time and money (travel expenses, mailings of magazines, long-distance telephone calls, and so on) before she ever realized any monetary rewards. Finally, this story proves that you should set your sights high; no prospect is too big to pursue. Although it is particularly difficult to get a foot in the door with high-profile people in the entertainment industry, Terrie was able to land the hottest actor in the movie industry before she had a single other client! As the saying goes, "Nothing ventured, nothing gained."

Terrie Williams formed her public relations firm, the Terrie Williams Agency, in 1988, when she signed up Eddie Murphy as her first client. With the magazine's permission, she continued to work at Essence *for six months while she moonlighted with her own public relations firm. Shortly thereafter, she ventured out on her own on a full-time basis. Some of her early clients were Miles Davis, Anita Baker, and* Essence *magazine. Other individuals whom she now represents are Sally Jessy Raphael, Janet Jackson, Sinbad, Russell Simmons, and Washington, D.C. mayor Sharon Pratt Kelly. Some of her corporate clients are AT&T, Disney, HBO, and Polaroid. Williams is the author of* The Personal Touch *(Warner, New York, 1994).*

EVERYBODY
IS A PROSPECT

Told by Judie McCoy

When I first started my career with Mary Kay Cosmetics, I was a homemaker with no sales experiences. I was told not to worry, that every woman who has skin is my potential customer or recruit. Over the past 18 years, I have come to realize how true these words are.

I became a Mary Kay beauty consultant in 1976 and have since worked my way to the top of my profession. Today I am a national sales director with several thousand beauty consultants in my own sales organization. Shortly after I became a beauty consultant, I began concentrating on selling the product line as well as recruiting people to sell in my organization. Our nickname is "The Real McCoys." I consider recruiting to be an area of selling that pays really big dividends.

As I learned during my Mary Kay career, if every woman is a prospect for our skin-care products, she might also be capable of becoming a beauty consultant—especially a woman who is enthusiastic about our product line. My success depends on recognizing women who are prime prospects for representing Mary Kay Cosmetics—many women who, ironically, don't appear to be good candidates. Let me tell you about a few of these surprising people.

Early in my career, in 1977, I had a booth at a bridal show in Milwaukee. Ginny Kumbera-Plutte, an attractive woman in the booth next to me, was selling Kirby vacuum sweepers. As a way of introducing Ginny to our products, I offered to give her a complimentary facial.

In a polite way, Ginny said she was too busy, but did add, "Here's my card. Would you mind giving me a call?"

I called her several times, and it was always, "Judie, this is not a good time. Call me in a couple of months."

Finally, six months later, Ginny scheduled her facial and arranged to invite a few of her friends to her home to attend what we call a Mary Kay skin-care class. Ginny loved the facial and our products, so I tried to recruit her to come to work for us. "No, not until two things happen," she told me.

"What are they?" I asked.

"First, I'm studying for my real estate examination, and I want to get my broker's license. Second, I want you to let me know when you make $4000 in a single month. That'll convince me there's money to be made in Mary Kay Cosmetics and that it's a good opportunity for me."

"Okay. When is your broker's test?" I asked.

"In a couple of months," Ginny answered.

This gave me a goal to shoot for, and sure enough, two months later, my monthly commissions were in excess of $4000. I called excitedly to tell Ginny: "I earned more than $4000 last month, Ginny. Have you passed your test?"

"You did! That's great!" Ginny said enthusiastically. Then there was a slight pause and she added in a disappointed voice, "But I didn't pass my broker's test."

Ginny took the test four more times before passing it, and when she did, I was one of the first people she called to announce her success.

"I'm impressed with you, Ginny," I said. "You set a goal to get your license, and even though you met disappointment, you didn't give up. You're going to be a real star in our field. I think you're ready to begin your career as a Mary Kay beauty consultant."

One year later, Ginny was a director and was awarded a pink car, one of the top prizes presented by Mary Kay Cosmetics to its biggest performers.

Shortly afterward, I was introduced to Gerrie Burley. Something seemed different about her, and later I learned she had spent 33 years as a nun. After leaving the convent, Gerrie took a job selling used cars. She had come from an unbelievably disciplined environment, out of touch with the "real" world as we know it. It looked like Gerrie had a poor background for selling anything, let alone cars or skin-care products. If ever anyone was a diamond in the rough, Gerrie was.

But Gerrie had a certain spark, and I responded to this feisty spirit in her. She is also one of the most caring and giving people I've ever known. True, she had much to learn, but what I liked about her was her eagerness to do whatever it took to do well in her new life. In short, Gerrie knew that she had to adapt to the world outside the convent and she did!

Gerrie became one of the top beauty consultants in my area and is still going strong, long after an age when most people retire. In many ways I learned more from her than she did from me. In particular, I learned a lot about people—and what a person of any background can accomplish if she is determined.

Kay Lee Castagna is another woman who didn't seem the type to become a Mary Kay beauty consultant. The owner of a BMW dealership, Kay Lee was used to working in a man's world; she had to be tough because many of her employees were mechanics and car salesmen. The first time I saw Kay Lee was at a lunch arranged by one of my consultants. Kay Lee was dressed in black polyester pants and a matching black sweater. She was about as far from the Mary Kay image of femininity and grace as anyone could imagine!

"I want to make money," she told me, "and I want you to teach me to be a lady."

I told her about the opportunities we could offer, and she said, "Now, let's get one thing straight right from the start. No way am I ever going to drive a pink Cadillac."

"First you have to see if you can win one," I replied. Then I asked her, "Why do you want to join our organization?"

Her motivation was to be part of a group in which she could make friends. She wanted support, and as she put it, "I want personal growth."

It was as if Kay Lee was telling me that, while she had attained monetary success and tangible possessions, she wasn't satisfied and was looking for more in life. What I truly enjoy about my career is "feeling" what somebody needs and tapping into those needs to help her achieve them. Both in selling and recruiting, you must create a relationship very quickly with people—I believe this is essential to succeed in all fields. I get a certain feel from my first contact with people and then I follow my instincts.

Needless to say, Kay Lee was an exciting challenge, but again, I saw a spark in her that I liked. To make a long story short, she became so successful, she sold her dealership and went on to become one of our top sales directors. And yes, Kay Lee loves driving a pink Cadillac.

Perhaps the most unlikely woman recruited in my area was Mary Krueger, who worked the graveyard shift as a deputy sheriff. When Mary finished her police work at 7 a.m., she would go home, sleep for a while, and then put her Mary Kay pin on her red jacket and conduct skin-care classes. A woman on the police force was an unusual candidate to be recruited into Mary Kay Cosmetics. Let's face it, it's unlikely that a woman doing macho police work would be selling cosmetics when she's off duty, not to mention operating on a few hours' sleep.

Today, Mary's favorite saying is, "Mary Kay got me out of jail." What did I see in Mary? Again, she was so eager to promote our product.

Exceptional prospects may not start out being so enthusiastic. In August 1986, I was conducting a training class at a consultant's home in New Orleans. She had invited some guests to attend as models for a skin-care class. One model, Debbie Cerise, seemed to be there almost against her will. In her thirties, Debbie was dressed in blue jeans, an old T-shirt, worn-out tennis shoes, and absolutely no makeup. Sitting there with her arms tightly folded, she assured us, "I'm only doing this as a favor. I have absolutely no interest in being a Mary Kay consultant."

Although I was concerned that Debbie's attitude might rub off on the other women present and ruin the night, I also looked at her as a challenge. Reluctantly, Debbie agreed to let someone give her a facial, and although she was hesitant to admit it, she finally admitted, "Gee, this feels good."

Two hours later, when Debbie looked in the mirror and saw how beautiful she looked, she was feeling much differently about herself and our products. At the end of the evening, I approached her and said, "Debbie, I think you'd really be good at doing what I do."

"Oh, I don't think I could," she said.

"Let me tell you a little bit about it," I replied.

Half an hour later, full of enthusiasm, Debbie said, "Yes, I can do this. I'm really excited!"

A year later, Debbie had worked her way up to a sales director, and has been driving a pink Cadillac ever since.

As I said, practically every woman is a potential prospect, even women, who, at first blush, appear to be most negative. This goes for slight acquaintances as well as long-time friends. Take, for instance, the time I was in a restaurant and bumped into a familiar face. "Excuse me," I said to a woman, "but did you happen to take ballet lessons in the fourth grade at Esther Moody Ballet Studio in Elm Grove?"

"Yes, I did. I'm Jan Schoenecker, and aren't you…"

"I'm Judie McCoy."

We made plans to have lunch, where I learned Jan was a sales manager for ITT.

When I mentioned I was with Mary Kay Cosmetics, she said, "Look, please don't bother me about your company; let's just talk about old times."

I smiled and didn't say a word.

"So you're wearing Mary Kay?" she'd ask, and I changed the subject.

This happened several times during lunch and finally Jan blurted out, "Okay, okay. Your skin looks better than mine."

"I know. Now don't you think you should try our product?" I asked.

"All right, I'll try the product," she said. "Say, Judie, do I understand you make a lot of money?"

"Yes, I do," I answered.

"You know, I've been working so hard and I feel I'm not going anywhere with what I'm doing."

"I know, Jan," I said. "Don't you think it's time you found out about Mary Kay's opportunity?"

"Okay, tell me about it."

A week later, she became a Mary Kay consultant. Today, seven years later, Jan is a director.

As you can see, I've sold and recruited a cross section of women ranging from a nun to a deputy sheriff. And naturally, there's a long list of housewives and professional women whom I have recruited into the business. Two include my sisters: Chris Jackson, who graduated with honors from Purdue at age 21 with a master's degree, and Cathy Halverson, whom we had nicknamed "Miss Volunteer of the Year."

Cathy had no interest in the business and had given my name to somebody to recruit me—that's how I was introduced to Mary Kay Cosmetics! And it was Chris who once said to me, "Oh, Judie, I am so happy you're doing something to get out of the house. But please don't bother me with this glamour and stuff because you know I'm a professional and a career woman." Well, after I gave our product to Chris on her birthday and she used it for two months, her attitude changed about what I was doing. Then when Chris saw how much money I was making, and her boss told her she was at the peak of her earning potential, her attitude changed too. To make a long story short, my two sisters both came aboard and have since become sales directors. I can't tell you how proud I was the first year all three of us won pink cars!

All too often, there is a tendency to prejudge people and consequently pass over many wonderful prospects. Judie McCoy makes a strong case that, yes, you can sell those people who appear to be most unlikely prospects. Judie emphasizes following gut feelings about people—when you sense something special in somebody, she advises, "go with it." Judie stresses a very valuable point expressed again and again throughout this book: *Super salespeople are able to quickly establish a rapport which enables them to build almost instant relationships with prospects.* In my opinion, this is not an innate talent but instead a quality developed over time through exposure to many prospects.

Judie McCoy began her career with Mary Kay Cosmetics in 1976 and has since risen through the ranks to the top of her field. Based in Waukesha, Wisconsin, she is currently one of 85 national sales directors who have reached this highest level of achievement at Mary Kay. This is a remarkable accomplishment considering there are more than 375,000 beauty consultants in this worldwide sales organization. Judie has won numerous awards during her Mary Kay career, including being twice named the number-one sales director and eight times seminar queen of unit sales. She is a six-time member of the Million Dollar Circle.

SELLING THE RIGHT PERSON

Told by Robert L. Shook

In 1989 I submitted a book proposal titled *Hardball: High-Pressure Selling Techniques That Work* to my agent, Al Zuckerman. In turn, Al sent it to a dozen or so editors.

With more than 25 published books under my belt at the time, I believed *Hardball* to be one of my better proposals. I was confident it would be quickly purchased by a publisher.

But one by one, the rejection letters came back. Several weeks later, Al phoned me from New York with the bad news. "You never know in this business, Bob," he consoled me. "I thought we had a strong proposal, but evidently I was wrong."

"No, you weren't," I disagreed. "It was a wonderful proposal."

"How good could it be if nobody wants to buy it?" he asked, sounding more like a philosopher than a literary agent.

"I understand what you are saying," I said sympathetically. A salesman myself, I knew my good friend Al must have been reluctant to tell me that the proposal was rejected across the board. After all, he knew I was excited about it.

"Because of my years as an experienced author," I continued, "I know when I do good work, and *this* is good work, Al."

"I have no doubts, Bob, but I'm not the one you have to convince. It's the editor who has to be convinced."

I thought for a moment about what he had said. "You just gave me an idea," I said, thinking out loud. "Most editors don't have sales backgrounds, do they?" Before he could answer, I continued, "And for the most part, they were English majors in college, and after graduation they came to New York to be assistant editors."

"That's a fairly accurate profile," Al concurred.

"Well, look at what we're doing, Al." I said. "Most people don't like being called on by salespeople, and they especially resist being sold when they sense somebody is high-pressuring them. Since editors have little or no business and selling experience, more than likely they don't rank salespeople high on their list of favorite people."

"Not many people do," Al said.

"So what can we expect when we submit to them a book on high-pressure sales techniques?" I questioned. "If they don't like salespeople, they probably despise *high-pressure* salespeople. And if this is true, we can surmise that they have no desire to edit a book on this subject. Nor, for that matter, do they have any desire to work with a high-pressure salesman turned writer."

"What's your point, Bob?" Al asked.

Knowing that publishing houses place significant weight on what their marketing people think about how well a specific book will sell, I said, "My recommendation is for you to submit the proposal to the vice president of marketing or the sales manager of a few publishers. I guarantee you, if that person is worth his or her salt, he or she will recognize *Hardball* as a winner. In fact, Al, if he or she doesn't say it's one of the best sales books written in the last 20 years, I'll eat the manuscript!"

"I'll supply the ketchup," Al joked. Then he added seriously, "Bob, I know exactly the person to read it. I'll send it to Larry Norton at Morrow."

Norton, a vice president and sales director, agreed to look at the proposal, and a few weeks later made an offer on *Hardball*. Zuckerman called to tell me the good news and to get my approval for the advance Morrow offered.

"Did he say it was the best sales book to come down the pike in quite some time?" I asked.

"He thought it was terrific." Al laughed.

"Because if he's not jumping up and down with excitement over it," I said, "let's find a publisher who is. I want people to believe in it as much as I do."

"So we'll accept his offer?" Al asked.

"Let's do it," I said.

Sometimes, within a particular company, a salesperson may give a sales presentation to the wrong person, and consequently, the hope of making the sale is greatly diminished. Often, it's a matter of having a soldier within the company who believes in what you have to offer. In this particular case, the soldier, or right person, was the vice president of sales who, from personal experience, knew that *Hardball* would be well received by salespeople. The agent wisely selected the "right" person within the publishing house to serve in this capacity. It is important to choose an individual who has the authority to "make things happen" for you; a weak soldier could weaken your sale. This advice also applies to selling consumer products such as life insurance, automobiles, and furniture. No matter how convincing your sales presentation, if you sell to the wrong spouse when the right spouse is not present, a buying decision is unlikely to occur. It is imperative to present your product to the person with the ability to say yes.

As a point of interest, *Hardball* went on to become a successful book in both hardback and softback. Published in several languages, it is currently a big seller as a six-hour audio cassette program produced by Nightingale-Conant. *Yet had the proposal not been presented to the right person, the book would have never been published!*

THEY CAN RUN BUT THEY CAN'T HIDE!

Told by Steven M. Finkel

In the early 1980s, I was founder and president of a major executive search firm headquartered in St. Louis. My speciality was placing executives with companies in the growing health-care industry.

A major Houston company that operated 175 hospitals was on my "hot list," so one day I decided to contact its management. My modus operandi was simply to pick up the phone and speak directly to the president. If I couldn't get through, I'd ask for the executive vice president, and if I still didn't succeed, I'd go down the list of the company's top management according to rank.

I have worked as a headhunter at every level of industry. However, when going after high-level positions, I have one cardinal rule: I intentionally avoid the person in charge of human resources. Let me explain.

At these levels, management generally doesn't *want* the personnel manager to know who's going to be replaced at the top echelon of the company. Moreover, even if personnel *did* know of an opening, it wouldn't have the specific detail I need to find the *right* candidate for the job. That personnel director, who doesn't have the authority to say yes, may even resist letting me talk to a higher-up manager who *can* say yes. So I avoid human resources. It's a lot easier to move down than to move up.

I never take a no from someone who can't say yes!

Well, I made my phone calls to the top executives at the hospital management company and failed to get through to anyone. So my next step was to follow up by sending a letter to the same executives. My letter simply introduced myself, telling these people: "I will call you to discuss ways we can improve the quality of your operation." Once more I struck out. This time I kept getting kicked down to personnel—it was not my most glamorous moment.

Still wanting to avoid personnel, I put my third approach into action. I started bombarding the same executives with mailings that provided information about their industry to which they were unlikely to be privy. The mailings included published articles, some written by me and some not, and even an occasional piece of literature about my company. Each mailing contained a personal note saying, "I thought this might be of interest to you."

At the same time, I started calling some of my clients who I thought might have some contacts with my prospect in Houston. After all, the health-care field is relatively close-knit, and I thought my clients might be able to get me in to see the president or vice president. Again, I made no headway.

If nothing else, I am tenacious. For an account with this potential, the more resistance I encounter, the more determined I become. As a boxing fan, I always call to mind what Joe Louis said before he fought Billy Conn for the heavyweight championship: "He can run but he can't hide." This was my exact sentiment with the hospital management account. I knew it was only a matter of time before I'd get my foot in the door.

My next strategy was to contact a few people in the company to find out who in upper management might have been recently let go. I discovered that the controller was no longer with the company. He reported directly to the president, the vice president of finance, and the treasurer—exactly whom I had wanted to contact!

I called the former controller, introducing myself as president of an executive search firm. "I specialize in securing key executives in the health-care field," I explained, "but before submitting a candidate, I check references with the former employer. Whom can I contact within your previous company to vouch for the quality of your work?"

He was anxious to accommodate me because, first, he recognized that I might find him a key position; second, he understood that my client companies routinely ask for references. So he immediately gave me the names of the president and the other key officers of the company whom previously I was unable to contact. I asked him to prepare them to expect my call. He did a great job!

This time when I called, I was immediately put through to the company's president.

After a brief introduction, I asked him a series of prepared industry-specific questions geared to the health-care field. These questions were worded so that anyone in the field realized I had a great deal of knowledge in health care. Moreover, the very specific terminology I used clearly showed my expertise. For example, "How creative was he in helping your hospitals to manage costs at a time when net revenues per patient are declining?" This question clearly indicated I knew the problems of hospitals, and the emphasis on *net* revenues per patient (not gross) would be particularly important to a president or financial person. Then I added, "With increasing competition from alternative means of providing subacute health care, how effective was he at increasing the bottom line?" These were classic industry buzzwords, again indicating knowledge of problems. Touching on a hot topic of the day, I asked, "How involved was he in establishing the overall managed-care strategy of the company?"

It became evident that I spoke the president's language and knew what was important to him. Mind you, these questions were *written out in advance*. Good preparation is an effective substitute for brilliance—and a lot more reliable!

From my scrutiny of the controller as a potential candidate, the president could predict how thoroughly I would prescreen candidates for his firm too.

After I established a rapport with the company's top management, I closed with an assumptive sales technique: "I almost feel a bit embarrassed," I said. "We specialize in working with companies in the health-care industry, as I expect you are well aware. We have heard from a number of sources that your firm has a need, but frankly I've been so busy, I hadn't got around to calling. What kind of position is that?"

I have discovered that it is the "American way" for people to want to reach out to somebody who needs assistance. By apologizing slightly as an opener, I generally get the reaction, "Hey, don't worry about it," and most people go out of their way to help. Second, by stressing, "We specialize in working with companies in the health-care industry, as I expect you are well aware," I imply, "We are the big guns in this field, and certainly you know this." Third, by saying, "We have heard from a number of sources that your firm has a need, but frankly I have been so busy..." I tell the prospect that I am quite active and therefore must be very successful in my work.

Finally, when I ask, "What kind of position is that?" I am *assuming* there is a position for me to fill within the company. And, of course, when the prospect tells me, it's an assumption that I'll be given the business—or why else would he or she be telling me?

As it turned out, the company was in need of a third-party reimbursement manager. Normally, this is a middle-management job, but for a firm that operated 175 hospitals, it was a key executive position. I did the search and ultimately secured the right individual for the position, which had an annual salary of $90,000. At 30 percent, my fee was $27,000. Once the new third-party reimbursement manager was on board, he needed a reimbursement specialist, and I recruited three excellent candidates with Blue Cross–Blue Shield to be interviewed for the position. One was hired, for which I received a $10,000 fee. About six months later, the reimbursement specialist was promoted to controllership of a small hospital within the organization, and I was asked to secure a business office manager for him. When the reimbursement specialist was promoted, of course I had to find another to replace him. All in all, for the next three years, I personally received annual fees from this account averaging $150,000. Later the firm was acquired by an even larger health-care company, and my services were used by both entities.

All this business came my way because I called the former controller, whose impeccable references enabled me to later place him in a high position. In that capacity, he became another repeat client, thus doubling the eventual results of this account penetration.

If at first you don't succeed in getting through to your prospect, try and try again. Steve Finkel demonstrates this lesson very well by his many attempts to sell his executive search services. After multiple conventional approaches, Steve came up with an innovative one—he called the prospect's former controller, and by asking him for references, was able to talk to the three key executives of the firm. In effect, Steve got in through the back door, but once firmly rooted, he generated a significant amount of business—sales that would otherwise have never been made.

Another valuable lesson is taught in this story: Make sure you see the person who is capable of making a buying decision. Steve wisely avoided speaking to the personnel director because this individual could say no but not yes. Too often, salespeople give a sales presentation to the wrong person, which accomplishes nothing and wipes out the chance to close a sale.

Note the sheer professionalism involved in this story. Steve Finkel mapped out his campaign like a battle plan. Ultimately, creatively, his entry to the prospect was smoothed by a third party. He *prepared* for his call, writing out the questions he intended to ask. Finally, with rapport and credibility established, he utilized a brilliant classical close, stimulating the prospect's emotions and improving his odds of success with every well-phrased sentence. This is superb selling. Steve's depth of knowledge of both "product" (his field) and sales technique is *typical* of the best performers in the profession. They master their business—totally!

Steven M. Finkel is president of Professional Search Seminars, a St. Louis training firm specializing in executive search, recruitment, and employment. The leading speaker and trainer in the field for over a decade, Finkel has conducted seminars throughout the United States, Europe, and Africa. He is the author of Breakthrough! How to Explode the Production of Experienced Consultants, *considered to be the definitive book in the search and placement industry.*

THREE

SELLING YOURSELF

Since there is no shortage of salespeople out there who offer either similar or identical products to those which you sell, it's important that you sell yourself. In short, if people aren't sold on you, they won't be sold on your product.

Unlike the old days when selling depended on a good gift of gab and a few dirty jokes over a round of drinks, today it takes much more to win over customers. Qualities like enthusiasm and conviction go a long way in making a sale and developing long-term relationships with customers. In this part of the book, you will see how some super salespeople do a terrific job at selling themselves.

LISTEN WITH SINCERITY

Told by Joe Girard

Years ago, I learned a good lesson when a man came into my showroom to buy a car. I spent half an hour with him and was convinced he was going to buy. All that had to be done was for me to take him into my office and write up the order.

As we walked to my office, the man started to tell me about his son, who was attending the University of Michigan. His face lit up as he spoke. "My son is going to be a doctor, Joe."

"That's great," I said. As we headed toward my office, I glanced at some of the other salespeople on the floor who were clowning around. I left the door open, and kept my eye on them as the customer continued to talk.

"Boy, is my kid smart, Joe," he continued. "I noticed how bright he was when he was an infant."

"Makes good grades, eh?" I said, still looking out the door at the guys on the floor.

"Tops in his class," the man said.

"What's he going to do when he graduates from high school?" I asked.

"I told you, Joe. He's studying at the University of Michigan to be a doctor."

"That's great," I said.

Suddenly, I looked at him and realized that I hadn't been paying attention to what he was saying. There was a certain look in his eye.

"Look, Joe," he said abruptly, "I gotta go." And with that he left.

When I got home after work, I went over my day and analyzed the sales I had made, as well as the ones I had lost. I started to think about this guy, and I had a bad feeling.

The next morning I called his office and said to him, "This is Joe Girard, and I'd like you to come back so I can sell you a car."

"Well, Mr. Big Shot," he said, "Mr. Greatest Salesman in the World, I want you to know that I bought a car from somebody else."

"You did?" I said.

"Yeah, I bought it from somebody who appreciated me. The other guy listened when I told him how proud I was about my son, Jimmy."

There was a silence, and he continued: "Joe, you weren't listening to me. You didn't think it was important that my son, Jimmy, will be a doctor. Well, let me tell you something, Mr. Big Shot. When somebody is talking to you about their likes and dislikes, listen to them. And listen with your whole body."

Instantly, I knew what I did, and I knew that I was dead wrong.

"Sir, if that is the reason you didn't buy from me," I said, "that's a darn good reason. I wouldn't have bought from somebody who did that to me either. I am sorry. Now I want you to know what I think, sir."

"What's that?" he said.

"I think you're a great guy. I think it's wonderful that you're sending your son to college, and I know one thing. I bet your boy is going to be the greatest doctor in the world someday. I'm sorry that you think I'm worthless, but do you think you could do me just one favor?"

"What is it, Joe?"

"Someday, if you could just come back and let me prove to you that I am a good listener, I'd like to do that. Of course, after the way I acted yesterday, I don't blame you if you never come back."

Three years later, he came back and I sold him a car. Not only did he buy one car, he sent dozens of his co-workers in and they also bought cars from me. And later, I sold one to him for his son, Jimmy, the doctor.

But boy did he teach me a good lesson. I never, ever again failed to give a customer my undivided attention. After all, one of the gifts God gives all of us is the gift of listening.

After that experience, I always made it my business to ask every customer who came in the showroom what he or she did for a living. Then I'd listen to every word he or she had to say. People love it, because it makes them feel important and it shows how much you care for them.

Sometimes I'd just say, "You know, I always try to find out, just by looking at somebody, what his or her profession is. No kidding. I bet you're a doctor."

This makes a guy feel important. "No, I'm not," he'd say.

"Then what do you do?"

"You won't believe this, Joe, but I work at the Milstein Meat Company. I slaughter cows."

"You know, I've always wanted to see that, George. Say, can you get me in there so I can see it?" And I'd look at the guy like he's the most important person in the world to me. Well, he'd be interested in me because I was interested in him. He'd think that he was doing something great. "Do you mean to tell me that you actually slaughter these animals and it doesn't bother you?"

"Naw, Joe, you get used to it."

"Oh, man, if I did that, it would bother me. Boy, I would like to see it. I really would. Do you think you can get me in? You can? When can I come?"

I'd pick out a time of the day when there wasn't much action going on around the showroom, and I'd go visit his plant. As we went through the plant, he'd introduce me to his co-workers and brag that I'm the guy he bought his car from. It gave me a chance to meet more people and sell more cars.

Then if another person came in the showroom who worked for another meat company, I'd say, "You know, I once sold a car to a guy who works at the Milstein Meat Company." By doing this, I was able to relate to the customer. "He took me through the plant, and do you know, I couldn't sleep for two days! Boy, am I telling you, that was really something else. Is it the same thing at your place?"

"Yeah, Joe, it's about the same thing."

"You're killing pigs though, aren't you?"

"Joe, we save everything with the pigs. Joe, we're even trying to figure out a way to save the squeal."

"Boy, I would really like to see that. I really would....How about if I come down to the plant between one and four on Thursday afternoon?"

Although most of us think of super salespeople as great talkers, we fail to realize that they are even better listeners. Listen to your customers. It shows that you are interested in what they do. It makes them feel important.

For 12 consecutive years, Joe Girard was a retail car salesman in a Chevrolet agency in Detroit, Michigan. During that period, he sold over 13,000 cars, an achievement that put him in the Guiness Book of Records as "the world's greatest salesman." Today, he is one of America's most sought-after speakers. He is the author of four best-selling books: How to Sell Anything to Anybody, How to Sell Yourself, How to Close Every Sale, *and* Mastering Your Way to the Top.

STICKING
TO YOUR
CONVICTIONS

Told by Bob Woolf

During Larry Bird's senior year at Indiana State University (ISU), he was being touted as the nation's best college player. NBA scouts were saying he would be a superstar in professional basketball. So Boston Celtics president Red Auerbach wisely drafted Larry the season *before* his last college year—a permissible practice in those days.

To avoid distractions, a committee of business leaders from the city of Terre Haute, where ISU is located, was formed at Larry's request to screen potential agents to represent him. The committee members included Bob King, the Indiana State athletic director; Lou Meis, owner of a department store and past president of the local bank; and several other leading businesspeople. These leaders simply had Larry's best interest at heart—they didn't want to see him be exploited.

Out of 65 agents on the original list, I was lucky enough to be requested to come to Terre Haute for an interview by the committee. At a local country club, the committee gathered around a long conference table, seating me at the head while everyone else sat on the side. For eight consecutive hours they threw all sorts of questions at me. "What would be an appropriate salary?" "How much, if any, should be deferred?" "Will there be a signing bonus?" "What would be the effect of inflation on a long-term contract?" "What are the tax consequences?" "How do you judge Larry's prospects for earnings outside his playing contract?" "What kinds of investment opportunities should Larry expect?" "Endorsements?" "Personal appearances?" "Money management?"

During the few months after this initial meeting, I received several calls from different committee members with additional questions. In time, the committee cut the field of prospective representatives down to 25, then to 15. Eventually, I was notified that I was one of three still being considered. This meant I was invited to visit Terre Haute for another round of interviews. This time, the seating arrangement at the table was identical, with one exception: At the opposite end of the table from where I sat, sat Larry Bird. He was dressed in overalls and sneakers. Larry shook hands with me upon our introduction, but he never spoke a word.

I had anticipated that there would be more talk about what I expected Larry's salary to be, so I came prepared. I brought the numbers on virtually every contract of every top athlete in America. When I began quoting salary figures, I emphasized the salaries paid to the Boston Red Sox stars Jim Rice and Fred Lynn.

Then, out of the clear blue sky, somebody asked, "What does Tommy John make?" The New York Yankees' pitcher was a Terre Haute native and until Larry Bird came along, he was the city's all-time biggest star athlete. It was evident that the man who asked the question wasn't the only one who wanted to know John's earnings. Heads turned to me and they waited eagerly for my answer. Before I could shuffle my papers, Larry, who had remained silent up until then, spoke out: "Mr. Woolf, Tommy John happens to be a friend of mine, and I don't particularly care to know what he makes…or have anyone else know what he makes."

I was very impressed with the character and integrity that this 22-year old college student exhibited by his statement. Following the meeting, Larry drove me back to my room at the Holiday Inn, and I mentioned that I admired his sense of decency and loyalty to Tommy John. He just shrugged. I could sense a chemistry between us, and I was almost certain that I would be chosen to represent him.

The phone rang shortly after I got to my room. "Bob, this is Lou Meis. Some of us would like to stop by to see you at the motel. Larry is coming too." I wasn't sure why they wanted to see me, and I anxiously waited to hear them out.

When they arrived, Meis served as the group's spokesperson. "Here's the situation," he began. "Our selection is narrowed down to you and Reuven Katz (a highly respected attorney in Cincinnati who represented baseball's Pete Rose and Johnny Bench). We have to know what you are going to charge as your fee for representing Larry. Will it be $10,000? $40,000? Give us a dollar figure. Mr. Katz gave us his number and now we need yours."

This was not the first time they had asked this question, and previously I was able to avoid answering it. It wasn't possible for me to even approximate a figure that far in advance. I had no idea how long the negotiation would take or what the actual work would involve. I explained to the committee that I did not work on a flat-fee basis. I have always worked on a percentage, with a maximum fee of 5 percent of the client's annual salary. The fairness of this practice has been upheld over the course of my career. This was the working relationship I had established with all my clients.

"I understand why this question is being asked," I told the committee. "I respect Larry's desire to know how much it will cost him. But I want to work with Larry the same way I work with everyone else. At the end of the negotiations when Larry has a contract, then we will agree upon a fee. I cannot give you a figure now. It wouldn't be fair to my other clients if I gave special treatment to Larry in order to get his business. Now it's no secret that I want to work with Larry. I consider this a special opportunity, but I just can't give you the answer you want."

Meis looked intently at me. "Do you understand the consequences?" he asked, meaning that if I didn't answer, there was strong reason to believe I wouldn't get Larry Bird as my client.

I nodded.

"Okay, then, I'm asking you again. Give us a figure and we can wrap this up. Chances are, I've got to tell you, that without it, you will not be representing Larry Bird. Now what is your figure?"

"I'm sorry but I can't do it. I can only repeat that my fee will be reasonable and I will work hard on Larry's behalf. But I will not treat Larry Bird any differently from anyone else I represent. I am prepared to accept the consequences."

We shook hands and they left. I knew I had done the right thing, but I wasn't feeling good about it. I called my wife, Anne, and told her what happened. Although she agreed that I did the right thing, I could hear disappointment in her voice. My teenage son, Gary, who had been listening on the extension phone, said, "It's all right, Dad. I'm proud of you. You stuck to what you believe in."

After I hung up, I knew I wouldn't be able to sleep, so I read for a while. About an hour later, there was a knock at my door. It was Lou Meis and Larry Bird. I invited them in, having no idea why they had come to see me.

"Larry would like to ask you something," Meis said.

"Mr. Woolf, will you represent me?"

"I would be thrilled to do so," I replied.

"Mr. Woolf, I have heard all about how tough Red Auerbach is. And I want somebody to represent me the way you stood up to us," Larry said in a soft voice. "You're the kind of person I want to represent me during my negotiations with the Celtic's president."

Bob Woolf stuck to his convictions and it won him a major contract with Larry Bird, who later became one of the all-time biggest stars in NBA history. A salesperson should never compromise his or her principles. Never, never, never.

Attorney Bob Woolf was founder and CEO of Bob Woolf & Associates, one of the nation's most successful sports and entertainment agencies. Headquartered in Boston, Woolf's agency is known today as one of the most prestigious and well respected in its industry. Sadly, Woolf passed away November 30, 1993.

SPEAKING
THE CUSTOMER'S
LANGUAGE

Told by William J. Bresnan

Back in 1967, I was executive vice president of American Cablevision, a cable company that was privately owned by multimillionaire Jack Kent Cooke and based in Beverly Hills. Our company had formed a partnership with a group of prominent local businesspeople in El Paso, Texas, to bid on their city's cable television franchise. After a few years of working on the project, the El Paso city council had narrowed down the competition for its cable franchise to three firms. Cablecom, General Electric, and our partnership, El Paso Cablevision, were the three remaining companies in the running.

The four city council members were scheduled to vote; the winning company would install and operate the first-ever cable system for El Paso. In the event of a two-two split, the mayor would cast his vote to break the tie. Our local partners were an attorney and two prominent businesspeople. They were astute and highly regarded leaders of the community, and in my opinion, terrific folks. They had previously informed me that three of the city council members appeared to be committed to voting in our favor, and accordingly, we anticipated winning the franchise.

Just before noon, however, on the day before the city council was to assemble for the vote, I received a call from one of our partners.

"Bill, you've got to get here right away," a panicked voice pleaded. "We think we lost one of our votes."

"Who?" I asked. "Who did we lose?"

"Sal Berroteran. He's the council member who owns the photography studio. We were counting on him and without his vote, we're dead. Bill, you've got to come down here immediately and get this guy back in our camp. If you don't, GE will get the bid at tomorrow's meeting."

"I'll be there as soon as possible."

I rushed home, packed my bag, and hurried out to the Los Angeles airport. On my flight to El Paso, I thought about all the time and money we had invested in this project over the last three years. Thousands of hours were involved. I personally made a minimum of 30 trips, and we brought in all those accountants, lawyers, and engineers. The expenses were certainly several hundreds of thousands of dollars. All this work—I kept thinking—just to find out if we could get the job. All that time and effort was now resting upon winning over Sal Berroteran, a local photographer.

It was late in the afternoon when my partners picked me up at the El Paso airport. In the car, I was told, "We've got to get you to meet with Berroteran so you can convince him to vote on our side."

At the small office we rented in El Paso, I called the photography studio and was informed that Berroteran had gone home for the day. However, whenever I called him at his home, I was told he was at his studio. I left my number at both places and when I didn't hear from Berroteran, I called again 15 minutes later. I kept repeating my calls to him, and each time, I'd get the runaround. Eventually, it became evident that he had no intention of talking to me. I was told he'd be home for dinner by 6:30 but when I called he still wasn't available. At 7 p.m., we determined that his vote was lost, and without it, we were out of the running!

None of us had eaten since breakfast. Although we had no appetites, we figured we should go out to eat and call it a day. On the way to the restaurant, an idea hit me. "What about J. Warren Hoyt? What do you guys think?"

"There's no use talking to him," the three of them insisted. "Pappy Hoyt is a definite GE vote."

"How do you know?" I asked.

"Look, Bill, we've gone over this a dozen times before," one of my partners said. "Our strategy has always been to get these three guys because GE has Hoyt. Well, now we've got only two of the three we were counting on, and there is nothing else we can do."

Pappy Hoyt was a retired electric utility line supervisor, a man in his seventies. Even though he was quite ill, he never missed a council meeting. He'd have somebody bring him in his wheelchair, but he'd be there, come hell or high water.

"Let's go over and see Hoyt," I suggested. "None of us are in a mood for dinner anyhow. We have nothing to lose."

"It won't do any good," one of them said.

"Yeah, but so what. The worst he can do when we call him is hang up. Let's give him a call and then we'll go to dinner."

Our team decided that I would be the best one to call Pappy, so we pulled into a gasoline station, and I dialed his number. He was home, so I introduced myself and asked if it would be okay for the four of us to come to his house for a visit.

"Sure," he said. "Come right on over."

When I got back in the car, I was told, "It's still a waste of time."

It was nearly 8 p.m. and dark by the time we arrived at his house. He welcomed us into his home and invited us to sit down at his kitchen table. "This is Bill Bresnan," I was introduced, "the president of American Cablevision Company, who's in from Beverly Hills."

"Oh, some big shot from L.A.," Pappy said.

"Well, not exactly," I replied. "Less than 10 years ago, I was climbing telephone poles in Rochester, Minnesota, after studying engineering for 2 years at Mankato Technical School. That's how I happened to get into this business."

"No kidding," Pappy said. "You're an engineer, and you climbed telephone poles." His face lit up. "I did too when I was a young man."

"You too?" I replied. "You climbed the poles with hooks on your feet too?"

"That's right," he said with obvious pride. "Say, maybe you can tell me how cable television works."

"Sure," I said. "What do you want to know?"

"Well, we got the telephone wires up there, and we got the power lines up there. How is it possible that a cable outfit can come along and string all these cables when the power lines are on the top of the pole, and the telephone lines are lower down?"

"We have to go above the telephone and below the power," I explained. "We do it all the time."

For the next two hours, I reviewed how a cable system works in conjunction with the power lines. As it turned out, nobody had ever explained the mechanics to him. The only things he was ever told were how cable television is marketed and the legal aspects involved. Every other cable person who talked to him presented a bunch of fancy proposals in a 3-inch spiralbound book. I recognized that he wanted to know about the nuts and bolts, which happened to be an area that I had some expertise in.

"Well, what happens if the cable television isn't working?" he asked. "How do you fix it without interrupting the telephone service? And how do you do it without screwing up the traffic and people's backyards?"

"Let's say we have a pole that's knocked down by a car," I answered. "If we get there first, before the telephone company people, we'll move the telephone wires out of the way to protect them. The same thing is true if they get there first, they move our stuff. We look out for each other in an emergency situation. Over a period of time, a camaraderie builds up between their crews and our crews. A really nice relationship evolves—it's almost as if we all work together for the same company."

It became obvious that Pappy had all sorts of doubts about cable television, and I answered every question he'd ask. About 10 p.m., I became worried about his health and said, "Look, sir, it's getting late and I don't want to wear our welcome out."

"No, no," he insisted, "I really want to talk about this."

We finally left his house at 1 a.m. As we headed to the door, Pappy said, "You've got my vote, young man," and he patted me on the back.

The next morning, just as we expected, Berroteran voted for GE, but with Hoyt's vote, we got the franchise. The GE lawyer came up to us after the meeting and said, "How in the hell did you guys get Hoyt?"

"We just talked to him," I said.

"But I had lunch with him yesterday," the lawyer said, "and he told me....I was sure we had him."

In my heart, I knew that it wasn't a case of the last guy who talked to him that swayed his vote. It was the new information we presented to him that was never explained before that did it.

Bill Bresnan's story illustrates how speaking the customer's language is vital in the selling process. By sitting down with Hoyt and talking to him as one engineer to another, Bresnan honed in on what a utilities engineer was interested in knowing about the cable television industry. As of this writing, in 1995, the El Paso cable system generates an estimated $3 million in monthly revenues, or $36 million on an annualized basis. After expenses, it is estimated that the annual operating profit—before depreciation, amortization, interest and taxes—is $18 million. The original contract has been renewed and expires in 2002. As a result of Bresnan taking the time to explain the nuts and bolts of the cable industry to Pappy Hoyt, over a period of 30 years, this one sale will generate profits totaling several hundred million dollars!

There is still another strong message to this story. As Bill Bresnan tells it: "We were within a fraction of a microsecond of not going to Pappy Hoyt's house, and if we hadn't we would have blown the whole deal. Although I give myself credit for being the one who made the call to Pappy, I must confess that I am embarrassed about how close I came to being talked out of calling him. Ever since, whenever things seem hopeless, I remember this story and I make sure to take the time and put in the effort to turn over that last stone. This applies to every salesperson no matter what his or her product is—you never know whom you're going to sell if you don't make the call."

William J. Bresnan went on to serve as president of Teleprompter. When Westinghouse bought the company in 1981 and it became Group W Cable, he served as its chairman and chief executive officer. In 1984, he started his own cable television company, Bresnan Communications, which is headquartered in White Plains, New York, and serves an estimated 180 communities; the company has recently expanded its operations to Chile and Poland.

MAKING
THINGS
HAPPEN

Told by Georgette Mosbacher

In 1990, after I sold my cosmetics company, La Prairie, I started Georgette Mosbacher Enterprises, a New York City–based company with a modestly priced line of beauty and skin-care products. The first thing I did in starting up my new company was to put my business plan together. Then I began the tedious process of sending the plan out to prospective investors to raise capital.

Investors were broken down into three categories. My A list consisted of people I thought would have an interest in making an investment. My B list were people I knew had resources, but I had no idea what their interest might be. My C list was made up of some really long shots. These were people I had met only casually or even perfect strangers—I knew they had the wherewithal if they liked what they saw, but the hard part was getting to them.

My modus operandi was to call a prospect two weeks after I mailed out the business plan and then try to set up an appointment for a personal meeting. One particular prospect was a Los

Angeles billionaire who made his fortune in the media industry. (He is reclusive, so I won't mention his name.)

Upon introducing myself on the telephone, I said, "This is a follow-up to the business plan I mailed to you."

"Yes, Ms. Mosbacher, I received it."

"If you have an interest in being an investor, I would like to meet with you in person," I told him.

"That would be fine," he replied. "When would it be convenient for me to meet with you?"

I couldn't get over how easy it was for me to make an appointment with him. A week later, I sat down with him in his spacious L.A. office to give my sales pitch. I came well prepared. I had all sorts of documentation, graphs, financial projections, and of course financial statements that showed how I, with a group of investors, bought La Prairie in 1988 and three years later sold it at a large profit. I was about halfway through my presentation when he interrupted me.

"Georgette, you can stop right now."

At first I interpreted his interruption to mean he wasn't interested. It momentarily took some of the wind out of my sails, but I wasn't about to give up and head back to New York without making a strong pitch.

A smile appeared on his face and he said, "I am prepared to make the investment in your company." He paused briefly and added, "You won't be needing any more investors. I'll invest whatever money you need."

Obviously I had a stunned expression on my face because he added, "Let me tell you why I feel this way about your business, Georgette. It is not actually your business I'm investing in. I'm investing in you.

"Two years ago," he continued, "I was walking through Bloomingdale's and you were on the floor selling your fragrance. I couldn't get over all the excitement you created. There was a large crowd of people around you, and the store was ringing up sales of La Prairie. Well, that told me something. I was very impressed to see a hands-on CEO who was selling the old-fashioned way. You were out there talking, feeling, and pitching your product, and it was obvious how much you believed in it. That's why I am investing in you."

He added: "I know you are the kind of person who makes things happen. You will go out there and do everything you have to do to make sure your business succeeds."

Before the meeting concluded, I had raised several million dollars—all the money I needed to launch my new company.

Top salespeople are successful because they are consumed with conviction about their company and product. They believe in it so much that everyone around them can't help but believing in it too. Their enthusiasm and conviction are contagious, as is Georgette Mosbacher's—which, I might add, is a particularly irresistible package that comes complete with charm and beauty. I imagine it would be difficult for anybody to say no to Georgette.

Georgette Mosbacher purchased La Prairie in 1988 and sold her company two years later when she started Georgette Mosbacher Enterprises. She is married to Robert Mosbacher, former Secretary of Commerce during the Bush Administration and chairman of the Houston-based Mosbacher Energy Company. A self-made entrepreneur, Georgette insists that not one penny of her husband's money is invested in her business.

A DIFFERENCE
IN CULTURES

Told by Jack Masser

As a Reynolds Metals Company sales representative, I was giving a sales presentation to a Japanese engineer. His firm was a designer of a machine that was to be installed at the Rouge Steel Company in Dearborn, Michigan. When completed, the machine would feed wire into a ladle of steel to be deoxidized. This is where I came into the picture, because Reynolds supplied the deox.

After several meetings with the engineer, I felt as though a nice relationship was beginning to blossom. At this particular time, our meeting was taking place in a trailer located on the site of the Rouge Steel's giant Dearborn complex. As I was expounding on the virtues of my product and the exceptional service my company would provide, a very attractive and shapely blond-haired secretary walked by. As she did, the engineer's head turned, and his eyes followed her from one end of the trailer to the other.

After she exited, I again had the engineer's attention. After a slight pause, I said in a friendly whisper, "You dirty old man."

"What that, you say?" he shouted with a strong Japanese accent.

"I said…" and I caught myself, realizing that although it was an innocent remark, I was in big trouble. For the next 30 minutes I did my best to explain that my comment was not intended to offend him.

In a similar circumstance, no red-blooded American male would have thought twice about being called a dirty old man, but I immediately realized that the comment had an entirely different meaning to a Japanese person. As a consequence, I had inadvertently insulted him. Not only did my explanation require 30 minutes of precious time, it nearly cost me the sale.

This is a fine example of how to talk yourself out of a sale! Masser is the first to admit that he erred in judgment by using an American colloquialism that was not transferable to Japanese culture. Colloquialisms should be avoided, because, even in the English language, many often do not "translate." An Australian or a Briton, for example, might take offense at an innocent remark made by an American. Likewise, a New Englander might not understand a colloquialism spoken by a Californian or a Texan. In short, the lesson is that you must be careful about what you say to people from faraway places.

Jack I. Masser is a successful sales manager for Alreco Metals, Inc. and lives in West Bloomfield, Michigan. Prior to joining Alreco, he was a sales representative for Reynolds Metals Company.

CREATING
A LEVEL
OF CONFIDENCE
Told by James McEachern

An old sales axiom dictates that good selling requires making your prospect feel confident in you or your company or your product. I take it one step further and say that if a buyer has confidence in all three, then making the sale becomes a piece of cake.

I have incorporated this into my initial approach to selling Tom James products. And for those of you who are not familiar with Tom James Company, we are a full-service clothier that calls on business and professional people at their homes and offices. We go to our customers and sell a full line of high-quality men's wear. One important advantage of our service is that it saves our customers time, since they don't have to go shopping.

One of the first things I say to a prospect is: "Mr. Smith, the reason I am here is that I want to be your clothier. I know that if you buy from me, it is because you are going to have confidence in me, my company, or my product. Well, I want to give you confidence in all three. So let me tell you a little about myself.

"I've been in this business for a long time. I've studied clothing. I've studied styling. I've studied fabrics. Consequently, I am confident that I am as good as anyone at helping you pick out a wardrobe that will be complimentary to you.

"My company has been in business for 28 years. We own all our shops. We've grown at a rate of more than 20 percent every year since we've been in operation. Some 70 to 80 percent of all our sales each month comes from repeat business. Our company is committed to serving people with all their wardrobe needs and being the best in our field. Now only you and our other customers will determine whether or not we are the very best. I am confident that if you try me, you will find that we are.

"In our product line, we have suits, sport coats, trousers, shirts, topcoats, formal wear—more or less everything that you can wear, I can supply. We make the best suits you can buy, and everything is made in our own shops. There is no one you can ever buy from who will give you the equal in price, value, and relationship. It is true that you can buy more expensive suits and you can buy less expensive suits, but when you buy in a similar price range from our company, you are going to get a superior garment. It doesn't matter if it's suits, sport coats, trousers, shirts, or any other product—in a comparable price range, we control the quality of our product and this is our competitive advantage.

"How does this sound to you so far, Mr. Smith?"

I have used this introduction for many years, and it always generates a positive response. I strongly believe that even when the customer has a level of confidence in my company and my product, he must also have confidence in me, or my chances of making the sale are greatly diminished.

Having a level of confidence also carries over to the customer's ability to make a good decision. For instance, on a recent call with one of our Tom James professionals, I showed several swatches of suits to a doctor. Before the doctor was told how much our suits cost, he picked out two and said, "I'll take this one and this one."

As an afterthought, he asked, "How much do these cost?"

After I quoted him the price, he became silent, and I could

see the blood draining to his head. I knew that unless I could gain his confidence and give him reasons that it was a good decision for him to buy two suits at a higher price than he normally paid, the sale was lost.

Having noticed in the parking lot that he drove a new Cadillac (his MD license plate indicated it was his car), I said in a low-keyed manner, "Doctor, may I ask you a question?"

"Yes," he replied.

"What kind of car do you drive?"

"I have a Cadillac."

"Well, what about the car you drove before you owned a Cadillac?"

"It was a Cadillac too."

"Let's go back still further before you owned one. What about before you drove Cadillacs?"

"I had a Chevrolet."

"Do you remember the anxiety you felt when you first went from a Chevrolet to a Cadillac...about the price?"

He immediately relaxed and said, "I understand." From this point on, price was no longer a problem and he bought the two suits.

Another thing I sometimes say if somebody balks about price is: "Let me ask you this. Are you a little bit concerned about whether the clothes are worth the price?"

The answer to this question generally is "You are correct."

"Do you buy the cheapest kind of car you can find?" I continue.

"No."

"What kind of car do you drive?"

After a prospect replies, I add, "So you pay a whole lot more than what you have to for transportation, right?"

"Yeah."

"Well, the same principle applies here. And once you buy higher quality, Mr. Smith, you will find that you will never be satisfied with lower quality again."

While I'm still on the subject, there are many analogies I can use similar to the one with cars, depending on what I see in a prospect's office. I might make a comparison with anything from the office furniture to the prospect's computer. The common denominator is that there is always something he paid more than was absolutely necessary to get above-average quality.

Another way I generate confidence in a prospect is by telling him a story about why a particular client buys from my company. "A couple of years ago," I say, "I sold some suits to a business machine salesman who was only an average producer at the time. The following year, he had risen to become his company's number-one salesperson.

"'To what do you attribute your success?' I asked him."

"'One thing,' he answered, 'is how I feel now that I've started wearing Tom James clothing. I feel like I am equal to anyone I call on, and now I never become embarrassed or uncomfortable about how I look. The big difference is the confidence I now have when I walk in to see somebody.'"

Still another story I might tell a customer is what I was told by Ben Weinberg who was president of the Atlanta Bar Association when I first called on him. Immediately after I made my presentation, he said, "Okay, I'm sold enough to try you out. Pick out two suits for me."

When I delivered his suits to him, Weinberg tried one on and said, "Okay, I like what you do and I like the suits. Every season from now on, I want you to come by my office and have the two suits laid out that you think I would most likely need. I want you to be in and out of my office in five minutes. Because what I like is not having to take any time buying clothes."

"By the way," I add. "Weinberg recently raised his standing order to three suits."

I've told my Ben Weinberg story many, many times. It's a very effective story because it creates confidence in somebody who is unsure about making a buying decision. This story reinforces the customer's belief that the service I offer is justified because of the time it saves."

Finally, if a prospect who is used to spending less money on his suits balks about the price of my product, I'll say, "Mr.

Smith, I know you're concerned about whether or not it is worth $150 more than what you normally pay. I know you have that concern, but I don't. I believe that once you wear our suits, you'll feel it's worth that much difference. And just to show you how confident I am, I'm willing to write you a postdated check for 90 days. Now, you'll get this suit in about 30 days, and then you'll have 60 days to try it out. If it wasn't worth the difference, you can cash my check. This way, you won't pay more than you normally do."

This has made numerous sales for me, and not once has anyone ever accepted my check. The response normally is, "Well, if you're that confident—" or something to this effect.

In conclusion, I always try to create confidence in my customer, because when a person has it, making a buying decision is easy.

Creating a level of confidence in the salesperson, the company, and the product is essential in every field. I concur with McEachern that people are unable to make a buying decision when they lack confidence. By the same token, decision making is not difficult when people are sure of themselves and believe they are receiving a good value in exchange for their money. In particular, I like how McEachern cites how people feel uncomfortable when buying a more expensive product than they normally do (such as a luxury automobile). He points out the uneasiness that accompanied his prospect's first Cadillac purchase after having previously owned a Chevrolet. This is a wonderful analogy that most people can identify with. After all, most of us have experienced the same apprehension and anxiety at one time or another after making an extravagant purchase.

McEachern's opening remarks about how he establishes a level of confidence before he presents his merchandise are superb. What he says is something every salesperson can adapt to selling virtually every product or service—and once down pat, the approach should be very effective.

James McEachern is the chairman of the board and chief exec-

utive officer of Tom James Company, a Nashville-based firm. When he joined the company 28 years ago, its sales were $170,000. Today, with a sales force of 364 representatives, Tom James Company's annual sales is in excess of $140 million.

SELLING
SPORTS
CELEBRITIES

Told by David Burns

I started Burns Sports Celebrity Service in 1970 after working as an account executive and, later, an account supervisor for several different advertising agencies. From my past experience and my desire to seek a new, challenging advertising role, I saw a need for a one-source service for agencies that hired sports celebrities to appear in advertising roles. At the time, such a company did not exist, so whenever a celebrity in sports was needed, the agency would have to track down the agent, contact the player's team, and so on. It was often a real time-consuming hassle.

At the time, I was one of the least probable people to start a sports celebrity service. I had never read a sports page in my entire life. I simply had no interest in sports. So when I approached my friends with my idea, they laughed and assumed I was kidding. And when they discovered I was serious, they asked, "What do you know about sports?"

While I have since learned a great deal about sports by the constant exposure I get in this business, it is not that knowledge that is the key to success in my field. Let's remember there are a lot of people around who are sports fanatics and know much more than I'll ever know. But they haven't made a living doing what I do.

The real secret to success in my field, and to so much in life itself, is to be truly trustworthy. Eventually, people will want to do business with you. I have always been aboveboard with sports celebrities and their agents—and with companies and advertising agencies that buy my services. Over the years, this approach has paid off for me in spades.

Let me tell you a little about how my business works. First, a TV commercial always starts with an advertising agency that wants a "talent." Never does it start the other way around with the client or corporation contacting me. Typically, an ad person known as a talent negotiator or business affairs manager (or some other title) originates the call to me. For the most part, however, I'm mainly brought in on the sticky or complicated cases. In this respect, I can be compared with a travel agency. Generally, you don't use a travel agency for a simple trip—but you do, for example, when you're going on an extended, complicated trip to Europe. You tell the travel agent: "Put me in a middle-class hotel. I want to fly over the cheapest way." Or you might say: "I want first-class accommodations, the best that money can buy."

In other words, you tell the travel agent to put together the best package to suit your needs. This way, you have to make only a single call and the agent does everything for you. Without the agent, you'd have to make dozens of calls to airlines, hotels, car rental agencies, restaurants, and so forth, and in all likelihood, you'd end up paying a little more for the same service. This is a good analogy to my company: You don't *have* to call us, but we'll just make it a lot easier for you when you do.

Now in order for me to be effective at what I do, little by little, I made contacts with all the major sports agents, and there are about 100 of them throughout the United States. This took some time, because when I first started calling on them, they'd say, "Well, I refuse to work through somebody," or "I'm not going to pay you a fee," or "I insist that the ad agency call me directly." But over the years, I received a decreasing number of rejections from sports agents.

At the same time, I discovered a frequent deception in this business. Many on the fringe of the talent business imply to ad agency executives that they are the "exclusive agent" for a star, when they simply are able to contact that talent. This has become my advantage, since I make no such claim. The Burns Service represents *those who need a sports talent,* not the talent!

At the same time that I was calling sports agents, I was pitching ad agencies. Since my background was at this end of the business, I already knew a lot of ad people, so I had a pretty good idea what they wanted. My marketing strategy was to be completely straightforward and totally honest with them so that over a period of time, they'd trust me for having their best interests when contacting a sports celebrity. Right off the bat, I knew my livelihood depended upon my building trustworthy relationships with ad people. I also knew that some of them were appreciative of my help, and others, much less trusting of my role. I had to make myself likable as well as expert.

Throughout my career, my way of building trust has been to be completely candid with everybody. For instance, when an ad agency calls me and says the project has a very low budget, I will tell the agency to call the celebrity directly. I won't be involved. Doing this has paid off, because, out of appreciation, most agencies call me the next time around when they have a job with a budget permitting my splitting commissions with them.

It's really such a small world, and after 23 years in the business, I've gotten to know everybody—not only the first-level people, but the second- and third-level people too. And here's another key to success: Treat the "backups" and secretaries as equals. Remember their names and interests. By building a solid reputation in the field, I'm able to get through to the right people with a single phone call. I can do in a few minutes what would take most others several involved phone calls—and my call, unlike others', will have a "solid" answer.

I remember a few years ago that a gold medal Olympian's agent ruined his own career because he lacked integrity. This well-known Olympian's very aggressive agent signed his client for many endorsements with many unfulfilled promises. Because of those "promises," sponsoring companies were willing to give long-term contracts. The agent burned all his bridges in the sports world, and even though he made a lot of money in the short run, he lost his reputation in his field.

Another thing that has worked in my favor is the fact that I was never star-struck. I wasn't dying to have lunch and dinner with sports celebrities, an expensive and time-consuming activity. Frankly I'd rather be with my friends! Even to this day, many people don't believe it, but I look at each of these celebrities as a product. I've been told by marketing people that this is one of my strong suits. I can look at them impartially, giving frank reports on their reputation and performing ability. This includes a negative in a talent's past which the agent would hide. Also if one star is overbudget, I can usually deliver an equally known replacement who's under budget—another example of my one call versus the ad agencies' many bewildering calls!

Don't take this as knocking the entertainment industry, but many of its people are too easily impressed by celebrities and quick profits. I have observed that when people are so infatuated, they tend to get greedy. They have dollar signs in their eyes when they look at their celebrity clients, and this inevitably comes home to punish the agent and his or her trusting client.

Over the years, I've also discovered that some of the biggest superstars have not let success go to their heads. Michael Jordan is a perfect example. While he is the greatest basketball player to ever play, I am convinced that he has true humility. As an example of his "excess humility," a few years ago Hanes Underwear was making a commercial and wanted Michael Jordan, Howie Long, and Joe Montana. Our agency worked on the schedules of all three, and lo and behold, when the shoot day came to make the commercial, Jordan didn't show up! I was stunned, because he is always reliable and never fails to show once he agrees. This time, however, he didn't call; he didn't do anything.

We finally discovered why when he apologized: "I'm just too shy. I feel uncomfortable being shot in my underwear."

The producer explained to Michael and his understanding agent that a revision of the TV commercial would be made which met their approval. Our agency also promised that he would be able to approve the storyboards, and if he really felt uncomfortable with the stand-in, we simply would not do any close-ups of the underwear unless it was out of the body—that is, the product itself. Finally, no stand-ins or close-ups were shot.

So you see, I'm always challenged, and with situations that are unexpected but often as curious as this one. The challenge is, of course, to keep everybody happy. And this, I believe, takes years of experience. And sometimes it means passing up some business and making less profit—but in the long run, I am rewarded.

It may sound old-fashioned, but integrity is essential for long-term success in the world of business. As David Burns illustrates, it is *the* key to his success. It's so simple, it's hard to understand how any salesperson could not follow this simple rule: *Always be flexible, but when it comes to principles, never, never be less than honest.* Of course, this means always doing the right thing—again, it is such a simple rule, it should always be automatic. It's when people try to cut corners or take a profit advantage of the other party that they do themselves harm. Your reputation can be your most valuable asset—guard it jealously. Study any of the successful salespeople in this book—or for that matter, any highly successful people in any field—and you'll observe that the ones who enjoy the *longest-term* success are highly principled individuals.

David Burns is the founder of Burns Sports Celebrity Service, located in Chicago. While others have tried to emulate his company, none has succeeded. Burns conducts his business so exceedingly well, he has literally cornered the market. Burns Sports Celebrity Service is truly a one-of-a-kind company.

THE LISTENER WHO COULDN'T HEAR

Told by Tony Parinello

In 1977, I was in San Diego, California, selling Hewlett Packard computers. Selling a product with a six-figure price tag is no piece of cake, especially back when many people had never heard of Hewlett Packard.

On an initial call, prospects would typically say, "Hewlett Packard? What's that?"

Others thinking of the old Packard Bell Company, wondered, "You still making those radios and TV sets?"

Then there were the wise guys who asked, "You still making those cars?" or "How's your football team doing?"

Selling computers for a company that had built its reputation in the field of oscilloscopes and testing equipment was no easy matter, and was even worse when I had to compete head on against IBM. Back then, IBM was synonymous with the word *computers*.

To add to the matter, I had what could be considered a really serious handicap. My hearing was so poor, I had to read people's lips in order to understand what they were saying.

Although I needed two hearing aids, at the tender age of 28, my vanity vetoed it. "Hearing aids are for old people," I had convinced myself.

Little did I know, my hearing impairment was working to my advantage. It became evident to me only when I called on Grady Robertson, founder and CEO of Robertson, Inc., a service bureau in San Diego specializing in running credit reports on prospective tenants for owners of large apartment complexes.

Now purchasing a computer system such as the one Grady Robertson was contemplating is not like buying a typewriter or a piece of office furniture. This installation would run a quarter of a million dollars, translating into one of biggest buying decisions Grady would ever make. Naturally, he wanted to make sure Hewlett Packard was the company that would best serve his needs; after all, in his industry, the company's computer is the heart and soul of the business. So, for good reason, Grady wanted to be absolutely certain to make the right buying decision.

I had made dozens of sales calls on him during the 10-month period I was trying to win the account, with many demos and presentations, frequent meetings, and numerous lunches. Indeed, it was a very long sales cycle.

In the meantime, competition was fiercely fighting to win the Robertson account. To my misfortune, one competitor was in the same business complex, just two floors down, and its reps were religiously at Robertson's offices.

What worked to my advantage was something I was doing unconsciously. Whenever I met with Grady, because of my hearing problem, I'd have to concentrate very hard so I could read his lips. To do this, I would sit on the edge of my chair, lean forward, and very carefully watch his lips move.

I did understand the importance of allowing him to have his own personal space. At the same time, I knew better than to focus only on a person's lips, because this makes the prospect feel uncomfortable. So I'd look at his whole face—his eyes, his jawbone, the wrinkles in his forehead, and so on. You see, like the spoken word, facial expressions convey clear messages.

Because it took every ounce of concentration I could muster to read his lips, my mind never wandered. It didn't matter if the telephone rang or a secretary entered the room—my eyes remained glued on Grady. The building could have caught on fire and I wouldn't have been distracted! Even when I took notes, I didn't take my eyes off him, because over a period of time I had developed the skill of being able to write without looking down at the sheet of paper.

Throughout the entire sales cycle, nothing ever distracted me when I was with Grady. Even when his secretary would come in and he'd make eye contact with her, when he looked back in my direction, my eyes were still fixed on him!

Now imagine what must have been going on in Grady's subconscious mind. I was sending the subliminal message: "You are the most important person in the world to me when I am with you." This approach works wonderfully. After all, isn't making your customer feel very special the exact message you want to communicate?

Evidently, my message came through loud and clear to Grady, because he chose my solution over everyone else's.

Upon receiving my commission check for this large sale, I decided to solve my hearing problem. So I went out and purchased two hearing aids! When I first wore them, they drove me nuts, because my brain picked up all sorts of noises I wasn't used to hearing. For instance, my brain would hear the sound my pen made on a note pad and ask, "What's that?" I could hear little noises like the one that your pants make when the legs rub against each other. There were thousands of little sounds I simply wasn't used to hearing, each of which was distracting.

I took the hearing aids back to my doctor and said, "Take them back. They're driving me nuts!"

"Look, Tony," he told me, "give it some time and you'll get used to them. Your brain will figure out that those are not important noises and it will ignore them."

I consented to give the hearing aids another try. That same week, I made a sales call on Grady Robertson.

The most amazing thing occurred—when I was in his office, I no longer had to sit on the edge of my chair in order to read his lips. I leaned back into my chair and, in fact, I even slouched a little. I took out my note pad and asked, "How's it going?"

Grady began telling me how the company was progressing with our new computer installation when suddenly his secretary walked in. Unconsciously, my eyes followed her across the room as I listened to Grady. Later, an executive entered the room, and again I lost eye contact with Grady. Although I wasn't aware of what I was doing, I was looking at every distraction, because now I was able to hear what was being said without concentrating on his face. "This is terrific," I thought. "I can look over there but hear over here!"

A few moments later, Grady stopped in the middle of a sentence; while I had been listening to him, I was glancing out the window. "Tony!" he said to me in a raised voice.

"Yes," I replied, turning my head in his direction.

"I want you to take them out."

"Take what out, Grady?" I asked.

"Your hearing aids."

Embarrassed, I asked, "Why?"

"Because I feel like you're not paying attention to me. I liked it better before, when you sat at the edge of your seat and watched my every move. You made me feel important, special. So would you please remove them?"

My face turned beet red, but I obliged him. I carefully removed my hearing aids and put them back into their case. After that, I had to get on the edge of my chair to hear him, and soon I was watching every move he made. And when I took notes, once again I never looked down on the paper.

A broad smile appeared on Grady's face.

This story clearly illustrates how important the skill of listening is in selling. Today, Tony Parinello remarks that people frequently tell him he is the best listener they have ever met—and the truth is *Tony can't hear without the use of his hearing aids!* Tony has since learned to sell *with* his hearing aids but realizes the importance of listening with the same degree of concentration that he did during his lip-reading days. "It's interesting," he points out, "that I can come out of a meeting with my associates with a much clearer understanding about what was said *because I listen so intently*. I'll sometimes say, 'Didn't you hear what so-and-so said?' or 'Didn't you see how he looked at you?' Then, I'll get a bewildered look and have to explain what I heard."

Of course, if your hearing is normal, it doesn't mean you can't concentrate like Tony does on what your prospect has to say. Just follow Tony's advice: "Listen to your customers as if you're hard of hearing and have to read lips." Listening carefully is one of the best ways *every* salesperson can win and influence customers.

Tony Parinello is the president of Parinello, Inc., a sales training and consulting firm headquartered in San Diego, California. He is a professional speaker and conducts corporate seminars and keynote speeches for many of the Fortune 1000 companies. He is the author of Selling to VITO (Very Important Top Officer), *which is also available on audiocassettes. Parinello hosts the nationally broadcast radio talk show* Selling Across America *on the Business Radio Network, aired in 107 markets across the United States.*

A LESSON ON LISTENING

Told by James Clayton

In 1981, after a 25-year partnership, my brother and I decided to get a friendly divorce. Since its conception, our Knoxville, Tennessee, company had grown from a hole-in-the-wall used-car lot to a $15 million enterprise consisting of a network of automobile dealerships and a manufactured-homes company. Essentially, my brother got the car business, worth about $7.5 million, and I got the mobile home manufacturing plants and retail sales centers, worth about the same.

Two years later, I decided to do a public offering for the manufactured-homes company. (Interestingly, the name of our product throughout the industry has evolved from "trailers" to "mobile homes" to "manufactured homes.") In the early 1970s, we had talked about an initial public offering (IPO), but because of the havoc caused by the OPEC oil embargo in 1974, the window remained closed for nearly a decade. During those years, there was no way you could take a company such as ours public!

In 1983, however, it was a different ball game. The market was boiling, the underwriters were swooping down upon us, and the vultures were circling over our heads. The market was pricey and I figured it was a wonderful time to do an IPO.

After meeting with a dozen or so underwriters, we went with Prudential Bache in New York and a regional firm in Nashville, J.C. Bradford. The two investment houses did an IPO for $31 million; I received a check for $10.5 million, while another check for $20.5 million was put into the company. Since I still owned 80 percent of the publicly owned company, I figure I did pretty well for myself. After all, just two years earlier, my half of the partnership had been valued at $7.5 million. [On October 18, 1993, *Forbes* magazine reported the value of Jim Clayton's 29 percent of Clayton Homes at $360 million.]

After going through the cycle of, first, being listed on the over-the-counter exchange, a few months later being listed on NASDAQ, and in December 1984 going on the New York Stock Exchange, I have become somewhat knowledgeable of regulatory requirements involving publicly owned companies. But prior to the initial underwriting, I was just plain naive. One day, a Prudential vice president said to me, "Say, Jim, what about your board?"

"Board?" I replied. "What board?"

"Well, you've got to have a board of directors."

"What does one look like?" I asked.

The local Knoxville companies I was familiar with put people like bankers, lawyers, CPAs, and ministers on their boards.

The Prudential executive explained that the New York Stock Exchange requires each listed company to have an audit committee comprised solely of directors who are "independent of management and free from any relationship that, in the opinion of the board of directors, would interfere with the exercise of independent judgment as a committee member." When the responsibilities of an outside board member were made clear to me, I realized that, in the best interest of the company, I needed a group of astute and prominent businesspeople to sit on our board. In turn, the board would provide a forum which I could not otherwise access. "No big deal," I said. "I'll just make a few calls to some good people who will do a terrific job on our board."

To accomplish this, I put together a list of about 30 names of prominent people I knew personally. After going through half a dozen or so names, however, I concluded that it wasn't going to be any easy task to attract the kinds of board members I wanted. While everyone was very polite, each apologized profusely and said no. The rejection I received ran the gamut:

"Sorry, Jim, but I'm already on too many boards."

"In today's business environment, there's too much exposure to a liability suit to serve on a board."

"My position with XYZ Company precludes me from sitting on another company's board."

"I'm not sure the public's image of the mobile home business would be good for my image, Jim."

I soon came to dread the inevitable question, "Tell me, Jim, who else has agreed to sit on your board?"

"Er, well, no one yet," I would answer sheepishly. We're just a small start-up company, and I'm just beginning to assemble a strong board. I have a nice long list of people I'm going to call, though."

Dial tone.

What I thought was going to be a piece of cake turned out to be far more difficult than I had imagined. Even though everyone apologized, and some even went so far as to flatter me, the answer was still no. They sidestepped me beautifully.

I concluded that I had to have a better answer for the uniformly asked question, "Who has already agreed to serve on your board?"

Obviously, it wasn't enough to say I had a nice list of people whom I was planning to call. I had to get one *big* player. I studied my list. Of the remaining 20 names, the most impressive person was Wallace Rasmussen. He retired in 1980 after serving as chairman of the board and chief executive officer of Beatrice Foods. At the time, Beatrice was a huge holding company with 450 subsidiaries, including Playtex, Samsonite Luggage, Airstream, Tropicana, Culligan, Dannon, Daytimers—the list goes on and on. Most of these subsidiaries were bigger than Clayton Homes.

Beatrice was headquartered in Chicago, but Rasmussen lived in Nashville both during his career and after his retirement. We had met before and he was familiar with our company because, for many years, he served on the board of Commerce Union Bank, a Nashville bank with which I had a long-term business relationship. This opened the door for me to call a bank officer, who kindly arranged a breakfast meeting between Rasmussen and me.

My sales strategy was not to ask Rasmussen to sit on my board of directors. Instead, I would ask his advice about going public. My entire presentation plan focused on asking him questions, keeping quiet, and listening to his advice.

My opening remarks were: "Mr. Rasmussen, I have never been in the public arena. Consequently, I know very little about it. I do know about your extensive business success with Beatrice and what you have contributed to the bank for so many years. So I would like for you to tell me what kind of board a company like ours should have. Perhaps you can elaborate on the kinds of people we should go after. And I'd sure like to hear your comments on how we should run our board."

Rasmussen got turned on answering these questions. He talked nonstop for the next half an hour while I just shut up and listened.

When he finished talking, I said, "Mr. Rasmussen, what you said is wonderful. This is just the kind of board that I would like to have. Sir, I wonder if you would mind helping me for a few months? Just to get it going?" And I shut up again.

He sputtered for a few moments and finally said, "Well, I guess a few months wouldn't hurt."

Since he had told me it was important to have a good audit committee with a good chairman, I asked, "Sir, won't you chair my audit committee for a little while? Just to get it going?"

He consented—ultimately serving more than 10 years on the board and various committees.

Salespeople think they have to talk a lot, but I have always espoused, "Sell, don't tell." And to sell, you have to listen. I learned this many years ago when I sold house trailers, and, of course, the same applies to selling other products.

"Which of your furniture items would you place along this wall?" I'd ask a prospect when showing our product. Then I'd just listen.

Or "Now the way this home would be positioned on *your* lot, describe the view looking out this window. When you're preparing your family's evening meal, will you be able to see the children playing as your look out your kitchen window as the sun goes down?"

Then I'd just listen, until I had my prospect mentally living in it. If a prospect has mentally adjusted to living in the home, it's easy to make the buying decision to physically move in.

Now back to my board of directors. I hardly spoke the morning I met with Rasmussen, and strictly by being a good listener, I reeled him in. He was such a big fish that some people shook their heads. They couldn't believe a little trailer dealer like me could get somebody like Rasmussen to serve on our board and chair the company's audit committee.

The strategy worked exactly as planned. Once I landed Rasmussen, I had no difficulty getting three other outstanding businesspeople to serve on the board. First there was Bill Lomicka, who was the treasurer of Humana. Lomicka was followed by Jim Haslam, whose privately held company, Pilot Oil, had $600 million in revenues. Haslam had served as campaign chairman for Tennessee Senator Howard Baker and as finance chairman for Tennessee Governor Lamar Alexander. Harvey Morgan, the managing general partner of Prudential Bache, became my fourth board member.

Jim Clayton explained it well when he said that good salespeople sell more when they don't tell. This message is told many times throughout this book, for good reason: It is a highly effective selling technique applicable to all salespeople in all fields. In this particular story, it worked successfully with Wallace Rasmussen, CEO of a multi-billion dollar corporation. There is another valuable lesson in this story: Notice that after getting negative responses when he first asked people to serve on his board, Clayton regrouped. Rather than "beat a dead horse," he changed his approach and decided to go after the big fish first, figuring that others would then be easier to reel in. Every salesperson can apply this wonderful lesson, especially when breaking in a new territory! *Go after the big prospect first! Once the big fish is your client, you can easily reel in the small fish. On the same note, the big prospect won't be "sold" just because you have reeled in a lot of little fish.*

James Clayton is chairman of the board and CEO of the Knoxville-based Clayton Homes, Inc., one of the largest manufactured-homes companies in the United States.

THE FOUR SEASONS IN LONDON

Told by Isadore Sharp

On our first trip to Europe in 1963, my wife and I treated ourselves to a stay at the famous Dorchester in London. Having been in the hotel business for two years, I thought the Dorchester the epitome of elegance.

Upon returning to Toronto, I happened to mention my wonderful experience at the Dorchester during a casual conversation with an acquaintance, who said to me, "That's a coincidence; my company owns that hotel." This gentleman worked for the McAlpine family, a major U.K.-based construction firm that has vast real estate holdings.

Without thinking, I quipped, "Well, if your company ever builds another hotel that fine, I want to be your partner." After saying that, I felt somewhat embarrassed, because the McAlpines were an old, established family in the United Kingdom, and I had only recently entered the hotel business. My father was a Polish immigrant who began in Toronto as a plasterer. Although I had grown up in the building business, I was just 33 and had previously operated a home construction company. And now, with two hotels in Toronto, I was suggesting that the McAlpine family be my partner in a joint venture!

To my surprise, my acquaintance actually conveyed my message to his immediate superiors in London, and a few weeks later he called. "Mr. Sharp, there is an interest. We've been working on a real estate project in London for about 10 years and haven't been able to get it off the ground. If you're interested..."

I gulped. "I am very interested," I told him. "I'd be happy to fly to London to talk to it over."

At my first meeting in the United Kingdom, I was told that the McAlpines owned a small site on Hamilton Place, located in a densely populated area of town. They had plans to build a moderately priced 320-room hotel on the lot. They figured a hotel with small rooms and cheap rates was the most feasible for the property.

"I would like to do business with you," I said, "but I want to build a luxurious hotel, something like the Dorchester."

"There are already too many hotels in London like the Dorchester," I was told. "There's the Connaught's Claridge, the Ritz, the Savoy, and the Grosvenor House. Another new hotel can't compete against existing ones. There isn't any way we can match their grandeur, so therefore it would be a dismal failure."

This was my first meeting with the McAlpines. Although we were at opposite poles on what kind of hotel to build, at least we had met. It was a beginning.

Several months later, I received an overseas call from Gerald Glover, a delightful gentleman in his sixties whom I came to admire and whose friendship I cherish. Glover was so typically British—almost the caricature of an English gentlemen in a play. His manners were impeccable and his dry humor, charming. He had a legal background, and watched over many of the McAlpine real estate holdings. He served as my liaison with the McAlpine organization.

"I'd like to talk with you, Mr. Sharp," Glover said in his crisp British accent. "Would you be interested in coming to London to meet with me?"

"Yes, sir," I eagerly replied. After a date was scheduled, I arranged to fly to London the night before. With the difference in time, I arrived in London at eight or nine the following morning. This was one of a score of trips I made over a long period of time to meet with Glover. Because I was in and out, nearly always in a day or two, my body clock never seemed to adjust.

My meetings with Glover were very social and unlike any others I have experienced during my business career. Lunch always ran around two hours. At times, it seemed as if he was more interested in getting to know me than in discussing business. After lunch, we'd go to his office or club and continue our conversation.

During one meeting, I explained that I thought a luxury hotel was bound to succeed. "This is a bustling city," I said to Glover. "On my drive into the city early this morning, it was as if people were coming from all directions into a beehive. Whenever North Americans travel to Europe, they want to visit three cities— London, Paris, and Rome." London in the 1960s was like New York in the 1940s, one of the most exciting cities in the world. It was inconceivable to me that a new modern facility would fail. Unfortunately, I had no surveys or business data to back up my feelings.

Over the next six years I made many trips to London, some only for a day. Glover called me every now and then saying, "You must come over to..." and I'd jump on an airplane to meet with him. Invariably, I'd return to Toronto under the impression that the McAlpines weren't interested, and say to my colleagues, "I think the deal is finished." Just the same, as long as they didn't say no, I continued to work with them.

On one particular trip to London, I again proposed to Glover that we build a 230-room luxury hotel, rather than the 320-room hotel with less expensive rooms that the McAlpines had proposed. "With the competition of the existing hotels," he answered, "we don't care to take the kind of risk you are proposing."

"I believe in what I propose so strongly," I told him, "I am willing to pay you the exact rent your firm wants for the 300-plus room hotel." I guess they thought me reckless when I added, "I'll bring my own architect to London to design what I want—a hotel with fewer but larger rooms, and, in addition, more spacious public areas. We will have a grand hotel!"

After this proposal, I was referred to as "the Crazy Canadian." To them, my proposal didn't make sense. Not one of their experts and consultants thought it would work. The general consensus was that London just didn't need another luxury hotel.

So again I returned to Toronto, and my colleagues commiserated with me. A little while later, Glover called. "I'd like you to come over to have lunch with some of my friends."

"You're asking me to fly over the ocean for lunch?" I asked incredulously.

"Well, I think before we enter into business relations, I would like my friends to have the opportunity to meet you."

"All right," I said. "By the way, who are your friends?"

"Just the Duke of Westminster and his advisers," Glover answered.

I arrived in London on the designated morning and was picked up at the airport. Our lunch was scheduled to begin at precisely 11:45 at one of London's private gentlemen's clubs in the city's financial district. Eighteen people were in attendance. Cocktails were served, followed by lunch. Afterward, everyone sat back in his chair to enjoy port and cigars. After a very long silence, one of the Duke's advisers turned to me and said: "Mr. Sharp, I know you have been invited here as our guest." There was a brief pause, and he added, "We would like you to tell us your views on some issues."

He then proceeded to give me three topics to discuss, including my opinions on Canadian Prime Minister Trudeau, the Canadian government, and my specific views on certain complex business matters.

I was dumbfounded. With no prior knowledge that I would be asked to speak on these subjects, there I was, the center of attention. So—I spoke. I have no recollection of what I said.

As we were driving back to the hotel, I asked, "Mr. Glover, why would you put me in that position with no warning about what I was going to say? Surely you realize I could have embarrassed you. These are your friends, and while I'll probably never see them again, you are going to have to meet with them and be held accountable for why you have gone into business with this young kid."

He said to me, "My dear boy"—which is how he had begun to address me lately—"My dear boy, that would not have been cricket." He smiled warmly and continued, "Besides, I have all the confidence in the world that you would not present yourself in a manner which would embarrass me."

Still, nothing tangible resulted from this particular trip. We continued to have talks, and there were still more trips abroad. Then one day, I received another memorable call from Glover. "My dear boy, I want you to bring your wife over, so we can meet her and have some discussions."

So Rosalie and I flew over to London. I felt very good about having her with me, because Rosalie is the most interesting person I know. She has an amazing facility to retain practically everything she sees, reads, or hears. Besides, she's a very creative person. In particular, Rosalie is articulate, and a charming dinner companion.

Rosalie and I were invited to a very formal dinner at Glover's town house. Rosalie was the only lady in the midst of this group of very proper British businessmen. We managed to get through dinner without too many mishaps, although I'm sure we must have used the wrong fork or spoon on several occasions.

After dinner, we adjourned to the parlor and, as usual, port and cigars were passed around.

"A cigar, Mr. Sharp?"

"No, thank you," I replied.

"Mrs. Sharp?"

"Yes, thank you," Rosalie said. She then took the cigar and placed it in her mouth.

I looked at her in astonishment, thinking to myself: "Rosalie has never even smoked a cigarette. Why in the world would she try to destroy the most important business deal of my entire life?"

The British are so polite that nobody in the room batted an eyelash. They acted as if this was normal behavior. My heart sank as Rosalie held the cigar out for the server to clip it for her. Then as he went to light it, she said, "No, thank you. I believe I'll keep it for later."

At this, everyone in the room broke into laughter, even me.

Rosalie was just being herself, expressing her sense of fun. Over the years, I learned that the British are down-to-earth people, so they appreciated her being so natural. As I discovered later, this was the reason for all the meetings over a period of six years. *They wanted to know what we were like before they would enter a long-term business relationship with us!*

So it turned out that all those trips to London paid off. We brought over our own architects from the Canadian firm of Webb, Zerfa, Menkes, and Housden. Together, they worked with the McAlpines' architects to build the Inn on the Park in London, a 230-room hotel that opened in 1970. The same year, it was honored as "The Hotel of the Year" in Europe. And the Inn on the Park has been one of the world's most successful hotels ever since. In terms of occupancy and rate, our hotel has been the leader among such competitors as the Dorchester, Claridge, Ritz, and Savoy—hotels that they had said we could never equal.

Several years after the Inn on the Park proved to be a success, I was having dinner with Sir Gerald [Glover had since been knighted]. I could not resist bringing up something that had been on my mind for a long time. "When you were representing your clients, and the final decision was yours, what gave you the courage to offer me that opportunity? After all, in those days I didn't have the wherewithal if things didn't work out. You were well aware that I didn't have the assets, and although I was guaranteeing to pay you rent, had I failed to meet my obligations, you would have had no recourse. After all, you can't get blood out of a stone."

"Negotiating with people over a period of time," he replied, "I've found there is only so much to be learned from a business perspective. To go further, ask somebody questions while you look him right in the eye, and get a sense of whether he can deliver. It's a sense you get when you deal with people."

Sir Gerald smiled at me and added, "This, my dear boy, you do on faith."

This story is a fine example of how conviction comes through in selling. It doesn't matter whether it's a brief half-hour presentation, or in this instance, one that takes place over a period of several years. Isadore Sharp believed in his concept of a modern luxury hotel so strongly that he was even able to convince others who initially opposed his idea. In a major business transaction which takes a long time to transpire and in which there is considerable risk, it takes more than a good gift of gab and a warm personality to consummate the deal. You must present concrete and dependable facts—and believe in them yourself. Only then does your conviction come through to convince others that you will deliver what you promise. As Isadore Sharp says, "It's not the balance sheet that people put their faith in—they put their faith in you. They trust you and rely on you putting your total energy and effort into making a deal work. That's what they're banking on—your belief and commitment."

Isadore Sharp, CEO of Four Seasons Hotels, Inc., founded his company in 1960. Today, the Toronto-based company operates 38 Four Seasons and Regent hotels, with 6 more under construction. Hailed by many as the world's premier luxury hotel operator, Four Seasons manages hotels around the globe—in Paris, Milan, Hong Kong, Bangkok, Singapore, Tokyo, Bali, Sydney, and other faraway places.

TAKING CHARGE

Told by Robert L. Shook

During a 1975 telephone conversation with Colonel Harland Sanders, founder of Kentucky Fried Chicken, I scheduled an appointment to interview him for a book I was writing titled *Total Commitment*. The 85-year-old entrepreneur agreed to pick me up at the Louisville airport so we could go back to his home to spend a day chatting about how he started his business at the age of 66.

"My flight arrives at 9:58 Friday morning," I told him.

"I'll be there," the Colonel said. "I won't know who you are, but you'll recognize me."

I had no doubt of that! I had read that Sanders always dressed in a white suit—just like he appeared in commercials and print ads. A caricature of him was on every bucket of fried chicken I had ever taken home—so there was no doubt I'd pick him out of the crowd.

I was looking forward to meeting Colonel Sanders. He was truly a man who had become a legend in his own time. The plane landed on schedule, and I headed directly to the airport's main entrance, where the Colonel and his driver were scheduled to pick me up.

I spotted him immediately. As I expected, he was wearing that white suit! He might as well have been wearing a Mickey Mouse costume. "What a great day!" I thought to myself. "My plane arrived on time, and Sanders is here waiting for me. Everything is going smoothly, just like clockwork!"

"Colonel Sanders," I said to him enthusiastically, extending my hand to greet him. "I'm Robert Shook."

"There ain't gonna be an interview today," the Colonel moaned. "I fell on the ice and banged my head."

"It's a real pleasure to meet you, sir," I continued, paying no attention to his comment about canceling the interview. "Gosh, I'm awfully sorry you hurt yourself."

"I fell on the ice this morning and gave myself a good bruise," he continued. "I had no way to contact you to cancel the interview. I didn't want to leave you here at the airport looking for me and me not showing up, so I stopped out here on my way to the doctor."

"That's fine with me, Colonel," I said, still ignoring the fact that he had again said the interview was canceled. Naturally, the thought of flying from Columbus, Ohio, to Louisville, all for naught, was foremost on my mind. I knew that if I didn't do some fast thinking, my "great day" would quickly transform into a nightmare.

"Yeah, that's quite a bruise," I acknowledged, looking at a noticeable bump on the back of his head. "Let's get going, and as soon as the doctor has you patched up, we'll head on over to your place."

Without giving Sanders a moment to speak, I turned to his driver and said, "Which way is the car parked?"

"Uh, over there," he pointed.

"Let's get going," I said, and started walking in the direction of the car. "We have to get the Colonel to the doctor."

The two men automatically followed me and the three of us headed to the doctor's office. After the doctor did some minor mending on the Colonel's head, we spent the rest of the day doing the interview. It turned out to be a wonderful day after all, *for both of us!*

When Colonel Sanders told me the interview was canceled, I

knew that only by taking control of the situation would I be able to save the day. So, in an inoffensive way, I took charge. A less experienced salesperson might have reacted more confrontationally.

After having the opportunity to get to know the Colonel, I'm confident that my approach was right. Suppose I had initially said to him, "Look, I flew all the way down here from Columbus, Ohio, to see you and my return flight doesn't depart until seven o'clock this evening. What am I supposed to do for the next nine hours?" I am sure that he would have replied, "It's your problem, Mister. Now I've got to get to the doctor." That would have terminated any possible chance of interviewing him. He would have absolutely turned me down. And had he done so, it would have been the treatment I deserved. Why? Because I would have been thinking only of my own self-interest—and that approach is poor selling. Instead, I chose not to make an issue of the fact that I had been told, "There ain't gonna be an interview today." By acting as though I didn't hear it, I was able to divert the Colonel's attention to another solution to the problem at hand. I would go with him to the doctor's office, and after he was treated, we'd commence the interview.

It was important to assume that my suggestion of going with him would meet with his approval. I did not wait for him to say, "Well, okay, you can come too." Instead, I immediately started walking toward his car, and as I anticipated, Sanders and his driver followed me. Consequently, it turned out to be a wonderful day for all.

INNOVATION

Interestingly, when you're asked to think about the most creative people, rarely will you put a salesperson at the top of the list. However, over the years, I have observed how super salespeople are among the most creative, innovative people I have ever met. Just how much so are they? As you read this part of the book, you will discover how innovative some of the better ones really are. They are so innovative, I am convinced that this is the principal quality that puts the most elite salespeople in a class of their own. It is this element of innovation that, in fact, adds a new dimension to their excellence. As you read on, remember to look for ideas that you can adapt to your own use.

CHANGING DREAMS INTO REALITIES

Told by Martin D. Shafiroff

A while back, I called the wealthy owner of a midwestern coal company from my New York office. I introduced myself and asked him a few questions about his investment portfolio. I was told he invested only in bonds; in fact, he had tens of millions of dollars in bonds.

"I'm very satisfied with my broker," he emphasized. "He's an expert in his field, and we happen to be good friends. Mr. Shafiroff, you are wasting my time and yours by trying to sell me equities."

"I have no desire to work with you in bonds," I replied, "because, at best, I am only mediocre in bonds. This being the case, I would rather not do business with you."

"I appreciate your being up front with me," he said.

"If bonds are your sole interest we may never do business. I refuse to offer you something at which, at best, I am mediocre," I said.

My comment seemed to take him off the defensive. He then elaborated on his successful coal company, which was evidently a great source of pride to him. We talked at some length about business in general. "What other businesses are you interested in?" I asked.

"You know, one of my dreams has always been to own a life insurance company," he replied.

"Oh, really?"

"Yes, life insurance is what I call a great business," the man went on.

"Well, who knows?" I said. "We may be able to do business after all. Let me go to my firm and see if the opportunity exists for us to start a life insurance company. If I come up with something that looks interesting, I'll get back to you."

"Now remember, I'm not into equities," he said. "But owning my own life insurance company—yes, that's intriguing. I'll look forward to hearing from you, Mr. Shafiroff."

After we hung up, I began researching the insurance industry. Before long I came across a life insurance company that was selling at a very low price after the company rejected a peaceful takeover bid. The stock took a big hit and was selling substantially below its book value—in fact, to the tune of nearly 50 percent. After I did my homework, I liked everything about the company. At that discount, I thought it a tremendous value. This company met all the criteria that my prospect had in mind for buying a life insurer. Everything, that is, except one. It was a publicly owned company, and he had no interest in buying equities. He specifically emphasized wanting to invest in a privately held company. This meant I'd have to convert him in order for us to do business.

My first step was to illustrate to him what it would take to start a life insurance company from scratch. I sent a letter to him with some documentation explaining how this could be accomplished. In my proposal, using a figure of $20 million for demonstration purposes, I showed how we could form a company for $20 million—and that would be our book value. But then we would have to set up sales offices, hire managers and salespeople, establish an office for processing, and then obtain an A++ rating from the insurance industry rating company, A.M. Best. I took him through all the steps. I estimated that all this would require between $40 and $50 million, including miscellaneous expenses. Even with that value of operations, I added, we would be only a regional participant until we built up enough capital and experience to become national.

I submitted this information to my potential client in a simple and direct package of correspondence. I waited a few days for him to receive it before I called.

"Did you have a chance to review the material I sent?" I asked.

"Yes," he answered. "You make it look like quite an undertaking."

"I've got a better idea," I responded. "There is a company on the New York Stock Exchange called the Life Insurance Company (fictitious name). It is selling at nearly one-half of book value! If we buy this company on the open market, instead of putting up $20 million for book value, we accumulate the same dollar amount for $10 million. We won't have to go through all the start-up procedures, hoping to get an A++ rating from A.M. Best. Why, the Life Insurance Company holds the highest rating already! We don't have to recruit a management team or develop a sales force either. And," I paused for effect, "we wouldn't be a regional, we would be national! Now the company is about 100 years old and is already well known. So we don't have to go knock on doors saying, 'We've been in business for a few months, and we'd like you to take a long-term risk with us.'"

I stopped a moment to let it sink in. Then I asked my question: "Why should we pay three times as much to create something when we can buy a public vehicle—that we could sell any time—and receive a high cash dividend while we are waiting for the results?"

Suddenly the man who had opposed owning equities saw the picture: the tremendous discount and value of going right into position with a public company versus the tribulations of creating a private company. After I showed him that equities could provide exactly what he wanted to accomplish, he no longer viewed the transaction as "playing the market."

During the telephone conversation, I sold him a sizable position, and over a period of time he accumulated more and more holdings in The Life Insurance Company. This excellent investment turned out to be the beginning of our long-term friendship. Over the years, I found other discounted bargains in which he took equity positions. He later told me: "Marty, do you know that my equity portfolio is now larger than my bond portfolio? Believe it or not, I don't view these investments as stocks. Instead, I view them as values. These are businesses that cannot be duplicated for twice the price."

This story demonstrates how a super salesperson must be resourceful and, through innovativeness, present his or her product in a way which fulfills the customer's needs. Obviously, the outcome of Shafiroff's cold call could have resulted in a quick "Good-bye, I am not interested." A lesser salesperson might have attempted to sell some bonds or, for that matter, make an all-out effort to get an on-the-spot presentation to sell equities. Shafiroff's fact-finding session enabled him to learn his prospect's dream—to own an insurance company. Then, after carefully doing his homework, Shafiroff was able to determine that owning equities in a public company would actually fulfill the prospect's needs. I believe that very few investment consultants would have taken this approach in spite of having the identical product available to them (since the company was listed on the New York Stock Exchange).

Martin D. Shafiroff is a managing director of Lehman Brothers. Based in New York City, he has been one of the nation's top-producing investment consultants for more than a decade. He has been written about in several books and featured in many business articles. He is also the coauthor of Successful Telephone Selling in the '90s.

LET YOUR SATISFIED CUSTOMERS DO YOUR SELLING!

Told by Barry J. Farber

In 1984, two years after graduating from college, I was selling Monroe copying machines. Although the company considered me to be a good sales rep, I believed I could do a lot better. A particular problem I was experiencing was selling to people who had never heard of Monroe. It was no easy matter going head on against Xerox.

After analyzing the problem, I concluded that if I couldn't differentiate what I had to offer from the competition, how could I expect anyone to buy my copiers?

I concluded that it didn't much matter what I said to the customer, because talk is cheap. Instead, I determined to come up with a way to show the customer the benefit of doing business with me rather than the competition. I asked myself: "How can I let my potential customers know I will provide them with such exceptional service that the value added will be more than enough reason to do business with me?"

Suddenly, a mind-boggling idea hit me like a bolt of lightning: *"I'll let my customers do my selling for me!"*

To do this, I called on customers with whom I had developed good rapport—these were the ones who were completely sold on me because I provided them with outstanding service. I asked each of them: "Are you satisfied with the service I have given you?" Once they said they were, I asked them if they would mind doing me a favor.

"Sure, Barry. What is it you'd like me to do?"

"I'd like for you to tell me what service I did that you liked in particular."

"Okay, Barry, what I liked most was…"

"Just a minute," I interrupted. "Do you mind if I get down what you say on my tape recorder?"

"Why no, I don't mind."

"You see, I want to play the tape for people who can't make up their minds about doing business with me," I'd say as I nonchalantly placed my tape recorder down in front the customer.

"No problem, Barry. Sure, I'd be delighted to say a few words." Then, pointing to the tape recorder, "Is that thing on?"

With the customer's cooperation, I'd ask questions such as: "How was the service *after* the sale?" Then I'd keep my mouth shut and let the customer elaborate on how wonderful it was.

"There were no problems?" I'd ask, realistically knowing that nothing ever ran so smoothly that something didn't go wrong, especially with a mechanical device like a copying machine.

One customer, a real estate broker, had once insisted I sign a paper stating that if her equipment ever went down I'd provide a loaner so her salespeople wouldn't get stuck on a busy weekend without a copier. A year later, I went back to her and handed her the microphone. She enthusiastically elaborated: "Our copier couldn't have broken down at a worse time. It happened on a Saturday morning and we were in a panic. Then I remembered Barry giving me his home number and telling me, 'If you ever need me, I'm on call 24 hours a day.' Sure, salespeople say things like that to make the sale, so at the time I took it with a grain of salt. But now I was frantic, so I called him. 'Barry, the copier is on the blink. Can you help me out?'

"Barry said, 'I'll be over in half an hour with a loaner. You can use it over the weekend until our service people can fix your machine early on Monday morning.'"

I can't begin to tell you how many times I've used that tape with prospects who were on the fence and couldn't make the decision to sign an order pad. You see, what people want most is to know that a salesperson will follow up and give them service when they need it. In the long run, that's what really matters to them. But nothing a salesperson can say convinces them, because customers think, "He's only saying that to get a commission." However, when they hear a satisfied customer say how he or she feels, it means a lot more.

The tape worked so well that I began taping customer's remarks that would work under many different scenarios. For instance, when a prospect was indecisive about whether to go with Monroe or another brand, I'd have a tape of my customer stating that our company gave so much better service than the brand they used in the past. Hearing an endorsement of this nature from an honest-to-goodness customer gave many prospects confidence to buy from me.

Another customer took our product over the competition's even though we were more expensive. When she heard several customers talking about the tremendous service and support they were receiving after the sale, she realized that the value of the service throughout the life of the product was worth the initial difference in price.

The tapes worked wonders for me, because they were so real. Notice that they weren't slick, like those expensively produced videos that many companies use—you know, the ones with actors and music in the background. My customers were down-to-earth, everyday common folks. My tapes had noises from machines in the background, telephones were ringing—there was nothing phony or insincere about them. They were the real McCoy.

I'd also get a reference letter from each person I interviewed to complement his or her audiotape. The letter confirmed the validity of the taped interview. I kept each cover letter in plastic and bound it in a looseleaf folder. Since most people won't take time to read a lengthy letter, I used a yellow reference marker to highlight a key sentence or two in the letter that supported what the customer said on the tape. Between the tapes and the letters, I had a powerful one-two punch.

Before long, I accumulated a "portfolio" of tapes to be used for the right occasion. Whenever one of my prospects expressed a concern over a particular problem, I'd say, "I want you to hear what so-and-so, who had the same problem, has to say." Then I'd flick on a tape and I'd shut up. I always knew that it was poor selling to knock the competition. When you bad-mouth a competitor, you're making yourself look bad. So instead of me making a negative remark, I'd casually push a button on my tape recorder and let one of my customers relate a poor experience he or she had with one of my competitors.

A majority of my tapes were endorsements by *my* customers, who raved about how I serviced them after the sale was made. Once my prospective buyers heard comments by satisfied customers, their fears would disappear because they were able to relate to the people on the tapes. Then I'd go into my close: "Why don't we go ahead with it?" That was my closing technique. It was so simple: *"Why don't we go ahead with it?"*

"Yeah, Barry, when can we get delivery?" a customer would say, as if he or she were reading from a script.

Barry Farber's sales soared after he came up with this marvelous innovative sales tool. It an inexpensive technique that can be used to sell any product. It is also effective in handling practically any objection. For instance, a prospect may say, "I'm not familiar with your company." And you promptly reply, "You know that's what Mr. So-and-So said. Here, listen to this," and you pop a cassette into your tape recorder and let Mr. So-and-So do your selling. As Farber illustrates, this technique works particularly well when you're closing a sale.

Barry J. Farber is the President of Farber Training Systems, Inc., in Florham Park, New Jersey, and in this capacity has trained tens of thousands of salespeople. He is the author of State-of-the Art Selling *(a Nightingale-Conant six-cassette audio program), and co-author of* Breakthrough Selling *and Diamond in the Rough.*

IT PAYS
TO ADVERTISE

Told by Richard Luisi

I first started selling Electrolux vacuum cleaners just before my first semester at Newark State College in New Jersey. At that time, July 1971, everyone in the company drummed up business by knocking on doors. Although I was just 18 years old, it didn't take me long to figure out I was working in a numbers business—the more exposure I got, the more product I'd sell. This meant I had to have my name in front of people so when they thought about buying a vacuum cleaner, they'd think about me.

My small car was my office. After being in the business for 18 months, I decided to purchase a van. I figured that since I went into battle every day, I'd do better if I had not only the guns but the ammunition too. I kept my van filled with several different models of vacuum cleaners, which included different canisters, uprights, and commercial machines. I also had an inventory of literature and supplies that included carpet shampoos, floor waxes, pads, bags, hoses, and brushes. This way, when somebody wanted to buy something, I had the merchandise to sell right on the spot. I didn't have to come back later when the customer might have cooled off.

Most important, I am a big advocate of having people know what I do for a living. To let everyone know, I put a big sign on my van reading: ELECTROLUX SALES AND SERVICE, RICH LUISI. My telephone number was included. My strategy was to let people see it so they could write down my number or, even better, pull me over to the side of the road. Then I'd have an opportunity to sell them. Back in the 1970s, this type of marketing was frowned upon by other sales reps. "People will spot your truck pulling into their driveway," they told me, "and won't answer their doors."

I thought differently. I believed service was so important in our industry that I wanted to be known as the "Electrolux Man" in North Plainfield, Summit, New Providence, Berkeley Heights, and Warren—the communities in central New Jersey where I worked. People would see my truck all over town and know I would be around when they needed service. Besides, I was very proud of my work—I had nothing to hide.

One evening, I attended a monthly kickoff meeting at the Holiday Inn in South Plainfield, New Jersey with about 50 other Electrolux sales reps. I was the only one with a van, and I remember that some of them poked fun at me for having it. The meeting ended at 11 p.m. When I came out to the parking lot, a woman approached me. "Is this your Electrolux van?" she asked. (I loved it—it wasn't a Dodge van, but an *Electrolux van!*)

"Yes, ma'am, it is."

"That's great," she said. "Do you sell Electrolux machines or do you just service them?"

"Just like it says, 'Sales and Service.' I do everything."

"Well, that's terrific. I am the manager of this motel, and I think I am interested in buying some machines."

That evening I wrote up an order for 13 units—at the time, the biggest order of my career. Service, supplies, and referrals continued for many years after the initial sale. It all happened because I did something different from what the average guy did. The news about my big order spread like wildfire throughout the company, and today the majority of Electrolux representatives drive vans.

Like other great salespeople, Rich Luisi dared to be different. Although selling out of a van doesn't seem unusual today, it was back in the early 1970s when Rich started doing it. Not content to be a run-of-the-mill salesperson, Rich was innovative in making himself stand out in the crowd.

Richard Luisi began his career with Electrolux in 1971, and 11 years later he was the company's number-one salesperson, quite an achievement within a sales organization of 15,000 representatives. Rich was Electrolux's top sales producer—National Sales Champion—again in 1985, 1986, 1987, and 1988. Over an 18-year period, he accumulated more than 35,000 customers for Electrolux. In 1989, Rich went into branch management and today resides in Marietta, Georgia, where he serves as Electrolux's Southeast Area Vice President. Rich was named Area Vice President of the Year for 1992 and 1993. Rich holds two company records which he achieved as a sales representative: 1104 sales in one year and an income of over $252,000 in a single year.

SELLING GLITZ

Told by Marc Roberts

At age 28, I acquired three 1988 Olympic boxers. My company, Marc Roberts Boxing, Inc., signed Ray "Merciless" Mercer, the 1988 heavyweight gold medal champion; Charles "The Natural" Murray, a junior welterweight; and Al "Ice" Cole, a cruiserweight.

I built a spectacular boxing facility in Newark, New Jersey for my fighters. I poured half a million dollars into a 13,000-square-foot warehouse and equipped it with a beautiful boxing gym with saunas and whirlpools, two boxing rings, and a state-of-the-art weight room.

Everything I put into the business came from my own assets—money I had earned after dropping out of American University at age 19. I made most of that money in real estate investments. Then I started investing money in my three fighters and acted as their manager. The three of them achieved a combined record of 49 wins and 0 losses in three years. Now keep in mind that 49 and 0 is impressive, but it works out to be 16 and 0 per fighter, and that's not quite enough to fight for the big purses. So even with their combined wins, my business was operating in the red. My expenses were tremendous. I had two trainers, two bookkeepers, a full-time strength coach, and a couple of gofers on my payroll. I also had to pay salaries to Mercer,

Murray, and Cole—plus I gave them a total of $150,000 in bonuses over the three-year period.

Before too long, I had more than $1 million of my money invested in the business, and I figured it would take another million to keep it going. I didn't want to liquidate any of my personal assets, so I thought, "Why not go to Wall Street and take my business public?" I named it Triple Threat Enterprises—obviously after my three fighters. Right at the start, I knew it would be a tough sale, because the company had never operated in the black. Furthermore, nobody had ever taken a boxing management company public before, and my timing couldn't have been worse. I did it back in November 1991, in the midst of the Persian Gulf War. Needless to say, the war was making the stock market shaky. Nobody on Wall Street was doing initial public offerings (IPOs), and here I come wanting to take three boxers public!

I was also doing something which just isn't done in the boxing industry—nobody ever puts money into a boxer until he starts making money. Nobody does because boxing is such a risky business. It is so difficult to figure out who is going to go all the way to the top and be the world's champion.

Knowing all this, I started putting my personal money into these three fighters at the very beginning of their professional careers. Now I wanted to take the business public. Not only had I managed a company that operated in the red since day one, but I wanted to do an underwriting for $3.5 million. This meant that every dollar to be invested in Triple Threat Enterprises would be purely on speculation, because there was no guarantee that the company would ever make money!

As you can see, it was no easy matter for me to sell an underwriter on doing an IPO on my company. Right off the bat I realized that in order for me to make the sale, I'd have to "package" my product in such a way that it would sizzle with sex appeal. To make it sizzle, I had a wonderful highlight videocassette produced that featured my three fighters. Naturally, the video featured only shots of them beating up and knocking out other fighters. I also showed them being interviewed, and again the cassette featured only the best interviews. Then I had some boxing experts give their "expert" opinions on how amazing my three fighters were. "It will be very unlucky," one of the experts said, "if Mercer, Murray, and Cole don't make millions of dollars."

After I put my "package" together, I recognized that I had to get only one person on Wall Street excited about my concept. That one person turned out to be Jack Dell, who was with F.N. Wolf, a small underwriter in New York City. I invited Dell to visit my boxing facility, and when he saw it, he was quite impressed. Of course, everyone who saw it was impressed. By the time I introduced Dell to my fighters and showed him the videocassette, he was drooling. His interest was in show business, and that's exactly what I was selling. It was glitz galore!

F.N. Wolf wanted a big piece of the investment for itself; consequently, the firm was not permitted to underwrite the IPO. Through the firm's contacts, we took the proposal to D. H. Blair, a major brokerage house which also had strong distribution capabilities. All in all, the underwriting generated $3.5 million. I received $1 million in cash—alleviating me of about $1 million worth of liability—plus a million shares in the company. The arrangement also enabled me to draw a large salary and even a big bonus. Later, I sold my remaining shares, and the total deal netted me close to $4 million.

What made the whole thing so interesting was what I was selling. *I was selling a dream!* Dell wanted to be in the entertainment field. Although some people don't realize it, professional sports is as much a part of show business today as is the Broadway theater or the movie industry. And the individual investors who invested $1000 or $2000 in Triple Threat stock were also buying a dream. They wanted to have a small piece of three fighters. And every time Mercer, Murray, or Cole got into the ring, an individual investor could say, "Hey, see that guy. He's my fighter." It was no different from placing a bet directly on one of the fighters. If any one of the three fighters made it big time, the investor's "bet" would pay off in the form of a higher price in Triple Threat stock.

Marc Roberts was able to identify exactly what he was selling. He wasn't selling an investment in a small company; he was selling a dream. Too often, a salesperson is unaware about what motivates his or her customer to buy. Roberts knew exactly what it was that got his customer excited. And that's what he sold.

Marc Roberts is the founder and owner of Marc Roberts Boxing, the forerunner to Triple Threat Enterprises. He resides in West Orange, New Jersey.

THE SURPRISE PACKAGE

Told by Clinton Billups

Early in my career, when I was still in my twenties, I owned a small advertising and public relations agency. To supplement my income, I sold memberships for the West Hartford, Connecticut, Chamber of Commerce. Selling memberships was a good tie-in with my agency, because it opened the door for me to meet business leaders in the community.

On one particular cold call, I stopped in on an owner of a small fabric store, a hard-working man who was a first-generation immigrant from Turkey. His business was located only a few doors down from the street that separated West Hartford from the city of Hartford. As it turned out, this was a bone of contention for the shop owner. About halfway through explaining the merits of being a member of the chamber, I found out why.

"Listen, young man," he said to me with a thick accent, "the West Hartford chamber doesn't even know I exist. I'm on the fringe of its business district, and nobody cares about me here."

"No, sir," I insisted, "you're an important businessman and we do care about you."

"I don't believe it," he maintained. "If you could show me just one bit of evidence to the contrary that I am included in the West Hartford business community, I will join your chamber of commerce."

At this point, I looked at him and said, "Well, sir, I would very much like to do that for you." I paused and added, "Can I make an appointment with you to come back?"

Obviously thinking this was an easy way to get rid of me, he said, "Of course, you can."

"Well, what are you doing in 45 minutes?" I replied.

He was astounded that I would want an appointment in 45 minutes. And taken by surprise, he simply said, "W-well, I'll be right here."

"Fine, then," I said, "because I'll be back in 45 minutes."

I quickly left his store and dashed over to the chamber's office. I picked up something there and stopped in a nearby stationery store to purchase the largest envelope in its inventory. Then, carrying this long, thin package, I headed back to his store.

I placed the large envelope on his display counter, and I began to reiterate what I discussed with him earlier. All during this time, his eyes kept looking at the envelope, wondering what was inside it.

Finally, not able to stand it any longer, he asked, "Young man, I don't have all day. What do you have in that envelope?"

I reached in and pulled out a large metal sign that the chamber had made up to place on every major intersection into West Hartford. I took him over to the window and said, "This is the sign that is going up at that intersection so the customers will know they are shopping in the exclusive West Hartford district. This is what the chamber of commerce is doing to let people know that you are in West Hartford."

A faint smile appeared on his face. I said, "Okay, now I've kept my end of the bargain, and you can do the same by getting out your checkbook." With that, he wrote out a check for his chamber membership dues.

That's when I realized that having a prop to take with me on sales calls is an effective way to get people's attention. Just imagine how you'd react if somebody entered your office carrying a nicely wrapped package! I've done this many times since. Once, for instance, I walked into an exclusive new restaurant in Simsbury, Connecticut, with a gift-wrapped package under my arm. I placed the package on the desk of the restaurant's owner, and for 20 minutes I pitched him on the benefits of having my agency handle his advertising. All the while, he kept looking at the package. Finally, his curiosity got the best of him and he blurted out, "When are you going to tell me what's in the package?"

"It's for you." I handed it to him to open. It was as light as a feather and inside was a foam rubber brick. A quizzical look appeared on his face and for a moment he was speechless.

"You know," I said, "building a business without professional advertising and public relations assistance is like building the foundation of a house with rubber bricks. It looks good but you don't have the proper support."

He thought about what I had said and broke out into a big grin. Then I signed him up as a client.

In a creative field such as advertising and public relations, having a prop is a strong selling tool. It is also helpful when you sell an intangible product such as insurance or securities. Besides, everybody likes a surprise, especially when it's a present.

Clinton Ford Billups, Jr., president of CFB Productions Inc., is a personal manager and television producer. Based in Riverton, Connecticut, he serves on the board of directors of the national Conference of Personel managers. His company manages such performers as Steve Kurschen, network television's "Mr Gadget;" Landsberg & Yount, duo pianists for the San Francisco Festival Pops Orchestra; "extraordinist" Craig Karges; Harry Freedman, "The Nation's leading Expert;" Jack Swersie, "That Guy with the Can of SPAM;" Travis Fox, "The Prince of Sleep;" and Jim Vicevich, syndicated television's "Money Answers" man. His television production credits include: Ordinary People—Extraordinary Powers; Kreskin's Amazing Mysteries, Kreskin's Quest; and his award-winning American Campus Tour, starring Emmy recipient Jayne Kennedy.

HOW TO SELL HOUSES BY A RAILROAD TRACK

Told by Tom Hopkins

I hadn't been in real estate very long when, in the mid-1960s, I made a memorable call on the owner of JBR Development Properties. The company had recently completed a housing development in Simi Valley, a small community northwest of Los Angeles.

The project consisted of 250 homes priced between $17,950 and $19,950. After several years, all but 18 of the houses had been sold. The unsold homes were all located on Rosalee Street—and as you can guess, something was different about them. These houses were a mere 20 feet from the fence that ran along a railroad track where a train came by three times every 24 hours!

Now the builder had already turned down my offer to represent him in the past, and my response was to bombard him with letters, but to no avail. "I have no interest in listing these properties with a residential real estate agent," he said again and again.

Several months later, while driving by his Beverly Hills office, I decided to see if I could set up an appointment with him. To my surprise, he consented to talk to me right then. The 18 homes were still unsold and evidently he was getting desperate.

He initiated the conversation by saying: "You're going to want me to lower the prices and have to give those houses away. That's what most of you real estate people do."

"No," I replied. "To the contrary. I'm suggesting that you actually raise the prices. What's more, I'll have those homes sold before the month is out."

"They've been sitting there for two and a half years, and you're telling me you'll sell them in a month?" he said in disbelief.

"Allow me to propose exactly how I expect to do this," I said.

"Be my guest," he said, leaning back comfortably in his desk chair.

"As you know, sir, whenever a real estate agent holds an open house, people can drop by at any time to view the property for sale," I began. "Well, we're not going to do things like everyone else. We will show the homes as a group, at the exact times during the day when we know the train will be coming by."

"Are you crazy?" he snapped. "The damned train's the reason we can't sell those homes in the first place!"

"Please allow me to continue," I calmly replied. "By establishing that the homes will be shown at precisely 10 a.m. and 3 p.m., we arouse people's curiosity. I propose that we put a big sign in front of the showroom home stating, 'SOMETHING SPECIAL IS IN THIS HOME. COME IN AND SEE IT.'"

His jaw dropped a few inches.

"Next," I continued, "I want you to raise the price of each home by $250, and then you invest that money in a color television set for each home." At the time, owning a color TV was something special. Most people still owned only black-and-white models. Incredibly, he agreed to my plan and bought 18 color television sets.

The train was scheduled to pass by Rosalee Street at five to seven minutes after the hour that each "viewing" was to be held. This meant I had only a few minutes to give a group presentation before the train came roaring by.

"Welcome! Come in!" I greeted people at the door. "I wanted you to arrive at this certain time because there is something unique about each of our Rosalee Street properties. First of all, I want you all to listen and tell me what you hear."

"I hear only the air conditioner," somebody invariably would say.

Naturally, my question generated some rather strange expressions from my audience. If looks could talk, they would have said, "What's going on here? What's this guy up to?"

"That's right," I'd answer, "but if I didn't bring it up, you'd probably never notice the noise because you're used to hearing an air conditioner. However, I am sure the first time you heard one, it distracted you. When you think about it, there are all kinds of noises that never bother us, once we get used to them."

I'd then usher the people into the living room and point to the color television set. "The builder is giving you this beautiful color television set with your home. He's doing this for a reason. He knows that when you live here, you will have to adjust for about 90 seconds, three times a day, to a sound you'll soon get used to hearing."

At this point, I turned on the television set, adjusted it to a normal sound level, and said, "Just visualize you and your family sitting here, watching TV." Then I'd wait until the train went whizzing by. For about 90 seconds, the house would rattle and everyone could noticeably hear it.

"Folks, I want you to know that a train passes by this house three times a day, for about 90 seconds, which is four and one half minutes in a 24-hour period," I said matter of factly. "Now, ask yourself: 'Am I willing to put up with this little noise—which I certainly will adjust to—in exchange for living in this beautiful home with a brand new, magnificent color television set?'"

In three weeks, all 18 homes were in escrow.

It is no wonder Tom Hopkins is the world's premier real estate sales trainer. His story brilliantly illustrates how a salesperson can turn a liability into an asset. Unquestionably, selling a house along a railroad track is an enormous disadvantage. As Hopkins points out: "When the JBR salespeople initially tried to sell the homes without mentioning the railroad track, every prospect knew it was there and had to be thinking, 'My goodness, look how close the railroad track is.' Then people would call to find out when the train came rolling by, and would be told three times every day. 'No wonder all the other homes sold but these are still here,' they'd say." By ignoring so obvious a liability, a salesperson makes his or her job considerably more difficult.

Never keep the disadvantages of your product a secret from the prospect. First, it is deceptive. Second, the prospect probably already knows, so omitting a pertinent disadvantage destroys your credibility. Anticipate every major objection before your prospect confronts you with it; then make it an advantage in your sales presentation. Emulate Hopkins and be up front with your prospects, and product weaknesses will turn into strengths.

Tom Hopkins is President of Tom Hopkins International, based in Scottsdale, Arizona. He is considered one of the nation's leading how-to sales trainers. The author of six books, his How to Master the Art of Selling *has outsold all other how-to sales books since its publication in 1980. Hopkins' latest book is titled* Low-Profile Selling: Act Like a Lamb, Sell Like a Lion.

SELLING SOLUTIONS

Finding a solution to your customer's problem(s) is a very persuasive way to make a sale. As you will observe, this approach is especially effective for selling big-ticket items such as hefty life insurance policies, computer systems, or large pieces of real estate. The stories in this part of the book illustrate how solving the customer's problem(s) generates incredibly big commissions.

THE
SUPERDOME
DEAL

Told by Randy Vataha

In 1983, six years after retiring from a career as a professional football player, I found myself back in the game—this time as a 50 percent owner of the Boston Breakers. The team was a member of United States Football League, a newly formed league that played in the springtime. Our original plan was for the team to play in Harvard University's stadium, which seats 42,000. When that couldn't be arranged, the team opened its first season in Boston University's stadium, which has a seating capacity of 19,000. Unfortunately, our breakeven point was 27,000 fans per game. It was obvious that we needed a different facility.

The Breakers finished with an 11–7 record, earning second place in the Eastern Division, and toward the end of the season we had sellout home crowds. Even with an ABC television contract to broadcast each of our Sunday afternoon games, the team operated in the red. There was no choice—without an adequate stadium, we had to leave Boston. After finishing the 1983 season, we started canvassing the country—visiting such cities as

Sacramento, Portland, and New Orleans—to see what facilities were available. Cliff Wallace, president of the Superdome in New Orleans, expressed an interest in having us lease the stadium, so I went down to see him. He indicated that the city was interested in attracting new entertainment. He added that the Superdome liked the idea of hosting our USFL team, since it played in the spring and wouldn't be going head to head with the Saints. Wallace also mentioned that there wasn't any major league baseball or basketball team in town, so a professional football team that played in the spring might very well work in New Orleans.

After our telephone conversation, I flew from Boston to New Orleans to meet with Wallace on a Friday afternoon in October. My mission was clear. I was loaded with information on the USFL, and I was going to sell him on why our team should play in the Superdome. With one successful season under our belt, I could demonstrate to him that the team had a good track record and was able to generate good attendance. Furthermore, we had finished only one game out of the playoffs, so the Breakers would come to town as winners.

Knowing that we were not going to draw 60,000 to 70,000 fans, even in a facility as choice as the Superdome, I understood our financial parameters. We had fairly tight restraints on how much of a lease we could afford. My first meeting with Cliff Wallace was scheduled the same night I arrived in town. I told him about what a USFL team could offer, and he elaborated on the Superdome story, describing all its great concerts and sports events. We agreed that it made sense for both sides to have the team move to New Orleans and play in the Superdome. However, before the agreement could be realized, we had to work out a lease.

This is where the deal became complicated. Wallace explained that under the Saints' contract, the Superdome received 10 percent of the gross revenues from ticket sales. The Saints also paid the game-day expenses, which included security, field maintenance, and whatever else it took to operate the stadium for the day. After hearing these figures, I quickly ran over our projections (based on attendance) and soon realized that we could not pay the 10 percent gross.

A fine gentleman, Wallace listened patiently and stated his position, which was honest, but definitely not a negotiating one. "This is what we are charging the Saints, and I don't see how we can charge less money to a new team," he reasoned. "How could we ever justify it to the Saints?"

I recognized that he had a legitimate point. Following a very pleasant meeting, we shook hands. On my way out, I said, "Let's meet again tomorrow in the afternoon. In the meantime, I'll talk to my partner, George Matthews, in Boston. If we both give it some thought, I'm sure this deal can be arranged." He agreed to meet with me on Saturday afternoon.

Our Friday meeting had ended so late that I had only a few hours on Saturday morning to do my homework. At this point, I knew it would take a real sales job to convince Wallace to lease the Superdome at a lower rate than what the Saints were paying. I understood very clearly that I had to come up with some solutions to his justifiable concerns.

I reviewed his position. The Saints had sellout crowds of around 70,000 for every game. Meanwhile, we figured our USFL team might get 30,000 fans a game, with average ticket prices about half of what the Saints' tickets went for.

That morning, I started to call around to a lot of people. For instance, I called some reporters at *The Times Picayune* and other local media people I knew so I could get a feel for the climate. One of the things I quickly learned was that the Saints had been complaining about what they thought was a one-sided lease. It was well known that they wanted to renegotiate it. The more digging I did, the more it became apparent to me why Cliff Wallace would *not* want to give our USFL team better leasing terms than what the Saints had. I talked to my partner, George Matthews, and the two of us concluded that we had to come up with some way to turn an obvious liability into an asset. That would be no easy matter!

It seemed as though everyone I talked to said the same thing: "Man, are you ever going to have a hard time trying to convince the Superdome people to give you anything below the Saints' deal. Because if the Superdome does, it will really have a problem negotiating with the Saints."

From past experiences, I knew it made little sense to tell Wallace, "Look, all I can say is we can't afford it. So either you take what we offer or we have to walk away." I didn't think Cliff Wallace and the Superdome people would have any sympathy for the argument that we couldn't afford it. That was our problem, not theirs.

I made a second round of calls, and asked the question: "Is it inevitable that the Saints' lease is going to be renegotiated, or is it up in the air?" After hearing everyone out, I concluded that a new lease was absolutely inevitable. It was also quite clear that the Saints had the Superdome management over a barrel. It was a given that the contract would be renegotiated at lower terms. This discovery gave me the ammunition I needed when I went back to meet with Wallace.

We met on Saturday afternoon. "I am familiar with your situation with the Saints," I told him, "and it seems to me that at some point you must acknowledge that your lease with the Saints must be renegotiated. To me, it would make a lot of sense if you could set a new standard at a lower number that the Superdome is comfortable with. Now I could live with 7 percent instead of 10 percent. So let's say you tell the Saints, 'Look, we now have a lease with a new tenant at 7 percent, and we're happy with it. This is a deal that could also be applied to your lease, and we would be happy to do it as soon as you would like.'"

Wallace listened intently, and I continued. "Cliff, I am suggesting that *you* set a new standard rather than waiting for the Saints to come back and try to renegotiate a lease at well below 7 percent. Because I assure you, they'll ask for a lot more than what I am proposing. Additionally, they're likely to want a big piece of your parking and your concessions and everything else.

"This is also a good opportunity for you to seize the public relations battle," I added. "By demonstrating to the media that you made a deal with a new franchise—one that the Breakers and the Superdome could live with—you're suggesting that it's a reasonable deal for the Saints too. Besides, you'll be showing the public that you're consistent by giving both teams equal treatment. This way, you could come out a hero. And you could set a level that you are comfortable with."

Keep in mind that during this whole presentation, I really wasn't concerned about the negotiations going on between the Superdome and the Saints. I was trying only to find a rationale for why the Superdome should lease us the facility for 7 percent. That was my objective.

Wallace was very straightforward with me. "It is inevitable that we are going to have to redo their lease," he confessed. "And what you say about setting a new standard makes sense. Your idea about our taking an aggressive posture has a lot of merit."

A little later, we shook hands on a New Orleans Breakers lease in the Superdome at 7 percent. "May I use your phone to call my wife?" I asked. "I want to tell her I'm not coming back to Boston and for her to start packing our bags to move down here."

Vataha's problem was that his football team needed to lease the Superdome but the price was too high. Rather than focusing on *his* needs, he wisely zeroed in on a problem that the Superdome had. He then built his sales presentation around solving that problem, not his own! Many of the most sophisticated sales are made by finding solutions to the other party's problems.

Randy Vataha was a star wide receiver at Stanford University. Upon his graduation in 1970, he played for the New England Patriots for six years. He finished his NFL career with the Green Bay Packers in 1977. In 1983 he became a 50 percent owner of the Boston Breakers, a USFL team. The following year, the fran-

chise moved to New Orleans. After the 1984 season, Vataha sold his interest in the Breakers and moved back to the Boston area. Today he is the chief executive officer of Bob Woolf & Associates, Inc., one of America's most successful and prestigious agencies for sports and entertainment personalities.

THE "EASY" WAY TO INCREASE YOUR ESTATE

Told by Barry Kaye

Recently I gave a sales presentation to a man with a net worth of approximately $20 million. As an estate planner, my objective was to sell him a life insurance policy so that upon his and his wife's demise, his heirs would be relieved of the burden of paying the tax obligation due on his estate.

"How would you like to borrow $10 million from your favorite investment banker at the cost of the interest on $2 million?" I started off our conversation.

A sophisticated businessman, he instantly responded, "I'd like that very much. But, Barry," he said, looking at me as if I had gone off the deep end, "who is going to loan me money on those terms?"

"At today's current rates of 5 percent, I'm talking about $100,000 in annual interest," I said.

Now I really had his attention. "What in the world are you getting at?" he questioned.

"Since you and your wife are both age 70," I continued, "it will take approximately $2 million on a one-payment life insurance policy, based on current assumptions, to obtain a last-to-die policy that will pay $10 million in proceeds."

"So, you see," I explained, "$2 million will produce $10 million, the amount of tax due on an estate valued at $20 million. We could borrow on your margin account, and you will be charged only $100,000 a year in interest for what is theoretically a $10 million loan."

"Well, at my age, I don't like to leverage," he said.

"With all due respect," I continued, "when you built your $8 million building, you didn't put out $8 million did you? You put out $800,000. And you did the same thing when you purchased your home. So every once in a while, leverage isn't the worst thing. However, in this instance, your $10 million portfolio is sitting at the brokerage firm and you have no loan against it.

"So I want you to borrow $2 million. With your municipal bonds and stocks just sitting there, you can borrow this amount just like that," I said, with a snap of my fingers. "Now, as a rule, you wouldn't want to sell $2 or $3 million of assets and pay capital gains tax to buy this policy, and I don't suggest that. I want you to keep all your assets intact. With an asset-to-liability ratio of 5 to 1, you don't have to worry about a margin call. Besides, if you thought you were going to get a margin call, you should immediately sell all your stocks. But with your muni bonds as a base, you needn't worry about that.

"Now, when you borrow the $2 million, you're never going to see it," I explained. "It goes right to the insurance company, and your loan is not due until death, when your portfolio is distributed to your children and grandchildren. Whether you and your wife live 30 more years or drop dead tomorrow, the insurance company produces $10 million.

"On the basis of what I just said," I added, "do you pay interest on $2 million or do you pay interest on $10 million?"

His eyes lit up with sudden understanding.

"I submit to you that you pay interest on $2 million, yet your children don't receive $2 million. They get $10 million.

"Did you ever get a $10 million loan anywhere for $100,000 a year interest?" I asked. "If you didn't do this, at your death your children would have only $1 million more in assets after taxes. Using my recommendation, they receive $10 million. And what is the differential? It's $9 million. What did it cost to receive this $9 million differential?"

"It cost $100,000 a year," he answered.

"Do you know any place you can put $100,000 a year, and when you and your wife someday die, promise me that there will be a $9 million return? In your circumstances, I don't think there is a better investment anywhere in the United States today."

"I agree, Barry," he replied.

"Now, if you need the $100,000 to live on," I added, "then forget it. If you have $20 million and you need the $100,000 a year I am taking from you, we'll forget it."

I paused briefly and said, "Since you're going to be dead much longer than you'll be alive, you're entitled to the rest of your life and even forget the children. But if you tell me that you have extra money—surplus, discretionary money—and that you can get the money from your brokerage firm, then why in the world aren't you doing this?"

My client looked at me straight in the eye and said, "That's a good question, Barry. Let's get it started as soon as possible."

This is one of the most innovative ways I have ever seen to sell life insurance. In a matter of minutes, Barry sold a $10 million policy—not bad in an industry that gives awards to agents who sell just $1 million in a period of one year. And you don't have to be super rich to benefit from this insurance concept. Barry pointed out to me that a husband and wife age 70 with an investment portfolio of $1 million could take out a $1 million policy and pay only $5000 in interest (based on 5 percent for borrowing $100,000 on margin). Barry thinks big—he added with a grin that it could also be done with a $100 million investment portfolio.

Barry Kaye is considered America's top life insurance agent. An expert on estate taxes, he is the author of Save a Fortune on Your Estate Taxes *and* Die Rich and Tax Free. *He is founder and chairman of Wealth Creation Centers, a firm specializing in estate tax cost discounts.*

SWITCHING GEARS

Told by Richard D. Schultz

At age 22, I started my collection agency, National Revenue Corporation. I had been in business for about a year when, in 1974, I interviewed Tom Speiss, Sr. Tom had a terrific track record as a sales manager, and I wanted in the worst way for him to join my small organization. Tom was a top marketing man, and I knew he was capable of doing a big job. But because I was so young and operating on a shoestring, Tom showed little interest when we first met.

"I'm telling you, National Revenue will someday be a giant company," I emphasized. "This is one of those once-in-a-lifetime opportunities for you to get in on the ground floor."

Tom didn't seem too impressed.

"Why don't you come with me on a sales call," I said in desperation, "and see for yourself how prospects react to the unique service we offer them?"

He agreed. To impress him, I looked through my date book and added, "Let's see now, I have an appointment to see BancOhio. How would you like to see how I work with a large bank?"

"I'd like that," he replied.

"Okay, be here at my office at 8:30 on Thursday morning and you'll come with me. I'm meeting with Al Harter, a vice president of the bank, at 9."

After Tom left, I started to get second thoughts about taking him to witness a sales call with BancOhio. After all, it was Columbus' biggest bank and the second largest in Ohio, and I had never opened an account with a customer anywhere even close to its size. In fact, if I did get a BancOhio order, the bank's business would dwarf my next biggest account. "Richard, you've really bit off more than you can chew," I said to myself.

For starters, it was even a fluke that I had been able to get an appointment with Al Harter. I did so as a result of being introduced to Wade Terry, a senior officer at the bank, whom I met at a social function. During my brief conversation with Terry, I told him about my company and asked him whom I should call on at BancOhio. "Al Harter is the man you want to see," he told me.

"You wouldn't have any objection if I mentioned your name, would you?" I asked.

"That's fine," Terry said.

I had already known that Harter was the main man to see if I was going to get any of the bank's business. I was told how difficult he was to sell, and one of the first things he'd ask me was for references. Since I was a brand new company, I didn't have any major customers who would impress him, although I did have some experience in my field because I previously worked for another company.

When I called Harter, I was prepared to deal with his first question, so before he could ask it, I said, "Wade Terry asked me to call you," and that's all it took to set up an appointment via the telephone. It was as simple as that to get my foot in the door. Harter asked a couple of minor questions and set up a time for me to see him. That, however, was easy compared with what I anticipated would follow once we met in person.

As the time approached for our meeting, I was beginning to feel a lot of pressure because there was so much riding on this call. First, I wanted to hire Tom Speiss as my sales manager; second, BancOhio was a holding company with 42 affiliated banks. I knew that if I could sell Harter, it would open the door to the other banks. In addition, it would do wonders for my business if

I could tell prospects in all those small towns where the banks were located that BancOhio was our customer. "What a wonderful center of influence the bank will be," I thought. I knew that simply mentioning it as a client would give National Revenue instant credibility with other companies. All in all, it was a very important sales call to me. As Thursday morning approached, I felt the pressure mounting and knew that I *had* to perform.

Tom and I arrived at the bank ten minutes in advance of my appointment, and at nine o'clock sharp we were ushered into Harter's office.

Harter was seated at a small conference table with three other bank officers. From the expression on Tom's face, I knew he was obviously impressed that I was able to set up a meeting with four banking executives. From past experiences, however, I knew better—using Wade Terry's name is what clearly generated the VIP treatment.

And though the bank executives were courteous and polite, Harter was by no means waiting with open arms to throw any business my way. Following a round of brief introductions, Harter barked at me: "I already have more collection agencies and billing services than I need, and I have still others who are waiting in line for a piece of the business, and they've been calling on me for years. They *all* tell me their firm is going to do a better job for me. What's so special about yours?"

For the next 45 minutes, I talked about the quality of the services we performed and the kinds of management information reports we furnished. I pointed out that, whereas Harter typically paid 33 percent of what an agency collected, we had a fixed fee per account option versus charging a percentage of the amount collected. In short, even though we did offer a superior service at a competitive rate, I realized that this by itself was not enough to convince him that we should replace his present sources.

Also mentioned during the meeting was how the bank turned over 10 percent of its collection business to outside agencies; the remaining 90 percent was worked internally at another location in a large bank building filled with bank employees. Once I was aware of this, I switched gears and focused on what the bank was spending to work its accounts internally. By doing so, I positioned myself not to compete with the other collection agencies, but instead to evaluate how the bank should be outsourcing. In essence, I compared the cost of doing collections internally against the cost of using our services on a fixed fee per account basis. As it turned out, not only would we do the job for substantially less than what the bank was spending internally, but we provided third-party authority. Anyone who is familiar with the collection industry knows, as did Harter, that a third party's batting percentage nearly always runs higher.

Once I knew I had his attention, I started putting up figures on his chalkboard. Rather than embellishing our services, I began asking him dozens of questions about his needs. I remembered what my father used to tell me about listening during a sales presentation: "Son, God gave you two ears and only one mouth," he'd say, "and that means you're supposed to do twice as much listening as you do talking." By listening carefully, I realized that one of Harter's hot buttons was his concern about how the bank's volume was growing at an alarming rate. It became obvious that in the not-too-distant future, the bank would run out of space to staff its work force. An even more serious problem was that the bank had a "lumpy workload," which meant that during peak periods it would typically have to staff up, adding as much as 20 percent more workers, and then, three months later, have to lay them off.

Now because recruiting, hiring, training, and letting people go is very costly, I was able to demonstrate how outsourcing could do a better job and for less money than what his department was able to accomplish internally. In effect, I was able to offer him what is referred to as "remote facilities management," which is a fancy way of saying we would do his work off site. Furthermore, I had positioned National Revenue as the "uncola" company rather than going head to head with all the other cola companies, which were competing for only 10 percent of his collection business and splitting it up among themselves.

My solution to his internal collection problem made so much sense to him that Harter agreed to have us do a 1000-account test on $3000 average-balance accounts for the bank. I was on Cloud Nine. At that point in my company's history, $3 million in placements at one time was the largest test run ever.

As it turned out, because we were serving as an extension of the bank's staff, the accounts turned over to us were fresher than the ones we normally received. Consequently, our yield was substantially higher than what we projected—and superior to what the bank was achieving internally. This meant that we were able to show the bank that we could outperform its internal collection efforts—and at a significantly lower cost.

When we received a contract from the bank, it was bigger than the combined sum that all the other collection agencies received. Eventually, we were given about 20 percent of the total of the bank's internal collections. (Keep in mind that the bank did 90 percent of its own collections and divided the remaining 10 percent among several other collection agencies.)

Several good things resulted from this sale. First, Tom Speiss joined our firm and served as a vice president for our company for more than 15 years. His two sons later joined our company, and today both are vice presidents with National Revenue. Tom Speiss, Jr. is on the West Coast and Lindsey Speiss is on the East Coast. As a direct result of my sales presentation made to Al Harter, not only did our company sign up BancOhio, but during the following several months we gained 41 out of its 42 affiliated banks, each independently operated, as our customers. And once we started telling other businesses in all the cities and small towns throughout Ohio that the local BancOhio was our customer, it became necessary for us to hire 10 representatives just to handle the leads that were generated.

Following our good experiences with BancOhio, we started going after more and more banks in all 50 states, and today, 9 of the 10 largest U.S. banks are our customers.

Richard Schultz's resourcefulness and innovation made what was otherwise a difficult sale. By conducting a fact-finding Q&A session with the bank executives, he was able to determine that the bank had a problem with its internal collections. Knowing this, Schultz was able to switch gears. Instead of selling his services in the same manner as one of many competitors already doing business with BancOhio, he demonstrated how his company could solve an internal dilemma faced by the bank. The result was a sale many times larger than would have been achieved under a conventional approach. At the time of the initial sale to BancOhio, National Revenue employed 20 people in its Columbus, Ohio, office. Today, the company has 32 offices with a work force in excess of 1200 people. As Schultz explains, "It was this sale to BancOhio that really put our company on the map."

Richard Schultz is the founder and CEO of National Revenue Corporation, one of the largest collection agencies in the United States. Today, there are more than 7000 collection agencies in America; National Revenue is one of the industry's Big Eight, with annual collection placements exceeding $2 billion.

CREATING A SENSE OF URGENCY

Simply put, when it comes time to make a buying decision, most people procrastinate. One reason people prefer to delay such decisions is that they are programmed to "think it over" rather than to give their consent to a salesperson. Either they simply don't like to part with their money because they're unsure of the value, or they are hesitant to buy out of fear of making a wrong decision. So by avoiding making a decision altogether, they can avert making a poor buying decision.

To overcome sales resistance of this nature, a salesperson must create a sense of urgency whereby the prospect realizes that he or she has something definite to gain by acting now—or something to lose by procrastinating! The stories told in this part of the book demonstrate how customers react when a sense of urgency has been created.

ONLY ONE CUSTOMER IS ELIGIBLE

Told by John Covell

Many years ago, while I was working as a sales representative for Xerox, we had a fellow on our sales team with a problem. It was the last week of the year, and Jim, who had had a good year, was still a few sales short of achieving President's Club.

At Xerox, President's Club was the highest level of recognition afforded a copier sales representative, and Jim was distraught that he wasn't going to make it. Our sales team met and decided to conduct a sales "blitz" of Jim's territory in upstate New York over a two-day period—*the last two days of the year*. We were committed to help Jim earn his President's Club recognition.

We worked in pairs and canvassed the territory for sales. We prearranged that, at the end of the two days, we would meet at a restaurant in a small town central to the territory. There we would turn in our sales orders to our boss and celebrate Jim's success.

It was 6 p.m. on the second day of our blitz when we all got together and tallied our results. Despite our efforts, Jim was still one unit short of the required level to achieve President's Club. All we needed was a single sale. It could be the smallest copier in our product line. But at Xerox either you made it or you did not. There was no recognition for being close.

"What a shame," one of the guys said. "Jim came so close, and we struck out."

"Yeah, who would have thought that, among all of us, we wouldn't have sold enough!" somebody else said.

"Just a bad break, Jim."

Soon everyone was saying good-bye and wishing one another a happy new year. "Just a minute," I said. "I've got an idea. You guys wait here for 20 minutes, and I'll be back with an order."

On my way out the door, I grabbed a rookie salesman and said, "Come on with me."

We were standing outside the restaurant and I told him, "There's only a few places open so go ahead and pick one."

"How about the pharmacy?" he replied.

"It's as good a place as any," I answered.

As we crossed the street and entered the store, I said, "I don't have time to explain. Just follow my lead."

He had no idea what I was going to do. I pulled a tape measure (standard equipment for Xerox sales reps) out of my briefcase and started walking up and down the aisles. I measured different areas, shook my head, and continued to do this until I caught the eye of the owner.

"What are we doing?" the rep asked me.

"Shh, be quiet and follow my lead."

Soon the owner approached me and said, "Can I help you?"

Acting as if I was deeply engrossed in my work, I ignored him and continued to measure.

"Can I..."

"I'll be with you in a minute, sir."

Then I turned to the young salesman with me and said, "I think there is room here, but I don't think this is the right business."

"You don't?" he asked.

"No, it's just not going to work."

"What are you talking about?" the owner interrupted.

"Let me explain," I said, turning to him. "Oh, by the way, my name is John Covell, and I am with Xerox Corporation. We are going to install a copier service in one of the businesses on this street, and we're in the process of selecting the one that will be the best for us." I continued to measure, and the pharmacist stood there with his jaw dropped.

"You see, sir," I continued, "we have to do not only what is right for that business but also what is right for Xerox. So we're trying to see which business that will be. When we make our selection, we will rent the machine to the company for X dollars, and the company will charge a dime to its customers for each copy made."

"No kidding," he said.

"Yes. I can see that you have the space here, but I just don't think you have enough traffic in this place to support it."

"Not so," he insisted. "I've got it. I have more traffic here than anyone on the street. You can't believe the number of people I get here. I have the traffic for this thing, and it would do great here."

"I'm not sure it's the right kind of traffic," I told him.

"Not so," he repeated. "I have a wonderful clientele."

"Well, I am willing to give it to you on a trial basis," I reluctantly said, "but I am just not convinced."

"I'm telling you I'll do it," the pharmacist asserted.

Ten minutes later, we were back in the restaurant with a signed order, and Jim made President's Club.

This is an excellent example of reverse selling. Instead of selling the customer, Covell literally reversed his role as a salesman and had the customer sell him on why his pharmacy qualified to lease the copying machine. When this sales technique is properly executed, the customer is put in the position of thinking, "Can I qualify for it?" rather than "Do I want to buy it?" With some imagination, this sales technique can be adapted to selling many different products.

John Covell is a former Xerox sales representative—and a past member of the President's Club. He was one of the top Xerox sales reps in the United States. Today, John lives in Cohasset, Massachusetts, and at age 43 he is vice president and general manager of the Herb Chamber Companies, one of the largest automobile dealership groups in New England.

WHEN AT FIRST YOU DON'T SUCCEED...

Told by John Covell

After spending a good solid hour with Bob Johnson, I was unable to close a sale on a copying machine.

"No, I'll just stick with my present copier," he said. No matter how much I talked, I couldn't win him over and get him to part with a few bucks.

It was an embarrassing situation because I was training a new rep, and we hadn't made a single sale that day. We walked out the front door, and I could tell that the kid was thinking, "Covell's a real bum." He turned to me and said, "Boy, this is tough, isn't it?"

"I'll tell you what we're going to do, kid," I said. "I want you to set your watch and in 45 minutes we're going to walk back into that office and write up that order."

"We're going to do that in 45 minutes?" he questioned.

"Absolutely."

We made a few more quick calls and in 45 minutes the sales trainee said, "Your 45 minutes are up, boss."

"All right, back we go," I told him. "It's time for Johnson Insurance Agency to buy its copier."

I walked into the office and said to the receptionist, "I've got to see Mr. Johnson."

"I'm sorry but he's busy," she replied.

Johnson's door was ajar, and I could see him sitting at his desk. I said in a loud voice so he could hear me, "I've got to see him right now. It is critically important."

"I really don't have time," he yelled from his office.

"Mr. Johnson, you've got to see me right now," I said in a loud voice.

He came to the door and said, "What in the hell is so important?"

I grabbed the trainee by the arm and we marched into his office. "Listen, Mr. Johnson, I just sold your copier."

"What do you mean?" he asked.

"The copier over there," I said, pointing to his machine. "I sold it. After we left here, I made a couple of more calls and I found the absolutely perfect buyer for it. You can't believe the amount of money he is willing to pay for that thing."

"Well, how much?" he asked.

I gave him a number, which actually represented nothing more than a small discount off the product we were offering. "But I have to have it right now," I said. "If I don't do this right now, it's all over."

"Well, what am I going to do for a copier?" Johnson asked.

"Can you get by for just the rest of the afternoon, because I will have your new machine here in the morning?"

He looked at his watch and said, "It's after 4:30, so I guess we can manage."

"Now I need you to okay these papers," I said, handing him an order blank, and I closed the sale.

Covell created a strong sense of urgency whereby the customer had to make a buying decision on the spot. In this scenario, the customer is put in a position in which he is unable to get the same deal (value, price, and so on). By not acting quickly, he stands to lose something.

This is John Covell's second story. His first is titled "Only One Customer Is Eligible."

GANGBUSTERS!

Told by Jay Bernstein

Back in 1965, I was no longer working for the William Morris Talent Agency and had formed my own public relations firm. I was just beginning to pick up major stars, such as Burt Lancaster, Sammy Davis, Jr., and Robert Conrad. One day I decided to call on Robert Culp, who at the time was starring with Bill Cosby in the television series *I Spy*. Although Culp did not know me from Adam, I burst into his dressing room, unannounced, like gangbusters and said in my most authoritative voice, "Culp, the name is Jay Bernstein with Jay Bernstein Public Relations. You better sit down and listen to what I have to say. *Your career is in big trouble!*"

Culp was standing there in his underwear in between sets, getting ready to change clothes. He had a stunned expression on his face. He was speechless.

I pointed to the only chair in the room and he sat down.

"Trouble? What kind of trouble?"

"Is Cosby around?" I asked in a hushed voice.

"We don't share this dressing room," he answered.

"Good," I said, "because as you know, there have been some rumors going around that the two of you are not getting along. And the way the public is hearing it, they are siding with Cosby, not you."

"It's nothing serious," Culp replied. "Is it?"

"Culp, if things continue on their present course, it won't surprise me if your career goes under."

"It looks that bad?"

"Yes, smack down the tubes. But I can turn it around for you," I reassured him.

"Coincidentally, I've been thinking about looking into hiring somebody to do my PR," he said, and stuck out his hand to shake mine. "I like your style, Bernstein. I need somebody with your kind of chutzpah."

I signed him up for $1000 a month, and we've been close friends ever since.

It takes chutzpah to pull off what Bernstein did—and when this tactic works, it works very effectively. He created a sense of urgency, and by doing so, he got Culp's immediate attention. It was this same sense of urgency that enabled him to close the sale. Bernstein presented a problem that needed immediate fixing—and he proved to Culp that he was capable of responding quickly.

Jay Bernstein has long been considered one of the top agents and managers in show business. During his distinguished career, he has represented an impressive list of actors, including William Holden, Suzanne Somers, Farrah Fawcett, and Linda Evans. He has also produced several movies and television series such as Mickey Spillane's Mike Hammer, *starring Stacy Keach.*

URGENCY!

Told by Mary "K" Kottich

December 13, 1993, started out like every other Monday morning since I gave up my teaching career 10 years earlier to sell real estate. Monday is the day all 45 of us at CENTURY 21 Mills First, Inc. in Seminole, Florida, tour newly listed homes. In groups of three to five, we pile into cars and "caravan" from house to house, familiarizing ourselves with properties for sale.

On this particular sunny day, our caravan pulled up alongside a beachfront condominium on Gulf Boulevard in Redington Shores, a tiny, quaint community just north of St. Petersburg. We all got out of our cars and met with the two homeowners. Then the tour began.

Members of our group were walking in, while others were going out. To an outsider, the procedure seems chaotic. But this is what we do, and it gets the job done! Admittedly, in a two-bedroom townhouse with about 1200 square feet, it gets a little crowded, particularly on the stairway, where we kept bumping into one another.

Since the house was my listing, I had a vested interest in wanting everything to run smoothly. As casual as we dress in Florida, all of us were wearing business attire, so when I spotted a middle-aged couple in warm-up suits, my curiosity was aroused. Who were those people?

Just then the seller said to me, "Mary K, you need to talk to those people over there."

"Who are they?" I asked.

"I'm not sure. They just walked in and started looking around when your group arrived. At first, I thought they were with your firm, but later I realized they weren't. I hope it's okay. I didn't do anything wrong, did I?"

"What do you know about them?" I asked.

"They're from Bluefield, West Virginia, and have been down here for a couple of weeks on vacation."

"I'll talk to them."

I greeted the couple with a "Hi, I'm Mary 'K' Kottich," and gave them a warm handshake.

"I'm Don, and this is my wife, Teresa," the man answered. "We were strolling on the beach and thought we saw an open house going on, so we dropped in to take a look. We didn't know…"

"No problem," I said. "I'm the listing agent on this property. It's a pleasure to have you here."

"Our car is right outside, and actually we're packed to go home to West Virginia in a few minutes. We've been vacationing in Florida for a couple of weeks."

"Here, let me give you some information on this property," I said, handing a package to Don.

"Isn't the view breathtaking?" Teresa said to me, looking at the beach.

"It'll be hard to leave here and head back home to all that snow and cold weather," Don commented.

"What exactly are you looking for?" I asked.

"Well, this is kind of like what we're looking for, but we really don't know what we want yet," Don said.

We talked about the condo for a few minutes and I answered several questions. "Tell you what," Don said. "Give me your card, and when we get back to West Virginia, I'll give you a call. Maybe we'll have you look at something for us."

I was just about to thank him, hand him my card, and let him fade away, when I suddenly thought better of it.

"No, no, I've got an idea," I answered brightly. "I'm on my way to my office, just a few minutes from here. Why don't you follow me there? You can just get behind me, and we'll go. I'll tell you how to get there. Just go up to the sign at the next exit on Gulf Boulevard, cross the bridge..."

Before they could say no, I made a beeline for my car, calling out, "Meet you at the office!"

Three of my associates were already waiting in my car, so, driving back, I told them what had just transpired.

"No way you'll ever see those people again!" one agent said.

"I think you're wrong on this one," I answered.

When we got back to the office, I saw a fully packed Cadillac in the parking lot with West Virginia license plates! "Now how did they get here before us?" I coyly said.

"Mary K, you're the luckiest person I've ever known," the doubting Thomas commented, shaking his head.

In my office, Don began to ask me a lot of questions.

He started off with: "How long has this property been on the market?"

"It had been listed with another agent for six months and now I've got the listing. The owners have dropped the price and it should move quickly now," I replied. I looked at Don's face. "Very quickly," I added.

"We want something on the water," Teresa said, "so we can step out of our house onto the beach and go for walks."

"Yeah, we've been walking on the beach and stopping in at some open houses," Don interjected.

"Off and on, we've been looking every time we come down here," Teresa volunteered.

"So you have your minds made up that you want a beach-front property," I said.

"Someday," Teresa answered. She paused briefly and continued, "Don is a stockbroker, and works very hard. He needs a place where he can unwind. That's why we come down here to Florida every year."

"But there's nothing like owning your own place," I added.

"Yeah, if we owned a second home, I'm sure we'd be here more often, and that would be good for Don."

"As it is, we just get away for two weeks every winter," Don explained. "Teresa's right. We should be spending more time down here. After all, you only live once."

"You're right about that," I interjected. "When people from up north own property in Florida, their whole life changes. They spend a lot more time down here, and you know what? I believe it adds years to their life."

"I couldn't agree more," Teresa said.

For a few moments Don didn't say a word. I remained quiet to give him time to think things through. He broke the silence with a question: "How firm are they in their asking price?"

"It was listed at a higher price with their former broker," I answered. "However, since they listed it with me, they dropped their asking price. At this price, I think it's a real bargain and, as I said, it should go very quickly."

"What makes you so sure?"

"For starters, when properties are priced right, the two kinds that go the fastest are the ones with beachfront views or those with golf course frontage."

"There's a whole lot of condos on the market down here, Mary K," Don asserted.

"That's right," I confirmed. "There's certainly no shortage of condos anywhere in Florida. What makes this one special is that it's a townhouse and has its own garage, so you drive right in, put the garage door down, and you're home. There aren't too many beachfront condos with their own garages. Also, you don't have to take an elevator up to your unit and walk down a long hallway like you do in a high-rise. What I personally like about this location is that you're on the beach and even within walking distance of some very good restaurants."

Don picked up a pen and a pad of paper from my desk. Again I kept quiet and let him think. He jotted down some numbers and handed a sheet of paper to me.

"I'll tell you what, Mary K," he said in a firm voice. "This is what I'm willing to pay for this property. Not a penny more. If they want to take it, that's wonderful."

I looked at the paper, and it was $10,000 less than the asking price.

"I'll need $10,000 in earnest money," I replied.

"No problem, I'll write you out a check. And if they accept, you don't have to worry about financing. I'll pay cash."

"Sign your name here," I said, handing him a contract.

After they both signed, I said, "Now don't you worry about another thing! Just give me your phone number in West Virginia, and you folks hop in your car and be on your way."

As they drove away, I looked at my watch. The entire transaction had taken less than 30 minutes. I pointed out to the sellers that it was a reasonable offer, particularly because there were no contingencies. The contract was accepted. Don and Teresa came back for the closing on January 31, during the worst weather in West Virginia's history; they were very pleased with their decision.

There are several lessons to be learned in this story. First, Mary K "seized the moment" by making a sales presentation to potential buyers rather than continuing with the caravan. Making the sale was her number-one priority; after all, that was the purpose of the caravan. Second, Mary K realized that if she allowed her prospect to call her from West Virginia, the odds were against her making the sale. Third, Mary K created a sense of urgency when she emphasized that, as a result of the reduced price, the property would probably sell quickly. Finally, Mary K understood that she had to close the sale while Don and Teresa were still in her office. As she explains, "Don and Teresa had no intention of buying a home when they woke up that morning. I knew if they got up and walked out of my office without signing on the dotted line and drove back to West Virginia, I would never see them again."

Mary "K" Kottich is a real estate agent with CENTURY 21 Mills First, Inc., a Century 21® franchise located in Seminole,

Florida. She entered the real estate field in 1984 after being previously employed as a third-grade school teacher. With 1993 sales production in excess of $20 million, Mary K was the number-one CENTURY 21 sales associate in Florida and ranked number four nationally for the firm. She is a member of the CENTURY 21 system's International Hall of Fame.

SEVEN

CLOSING
THE SALE

Nothing happens until a sale is closed. No matter how well you otherwise perform during a sales presentation, if you walk out the door without an order, you failed to do your job!

Putting things in their proper perspective, your number-one objective as a salesperson is to close sales. Without closing the sale, neither you nor the prospect benefits. So, for good reason, being a good closer is crucial to your career as a salesperson.

Although closing the sale is the most important part of the selling process, it is in this area that salespeople are least likely to excel. So, understandably, salespeople are constantly seeking techniques to make them more proficient in closing sales. This part of the book contains stories about how difficult sales were closed. Each of these closing techniques has been field-tested—and works. None are hypothetical. Read them and try them out on your own.

SELLING THE
HOUSTON ASTROS

Told by William E. Odom

In December 1978, as an upper-middle manager of Ford Motor Credit Company, I was sent to Texas with a most unusual assignment: My mission was to sell the Houston Astros, the team's 99-year lease on the Astrodome, and everything that comes with the ballpark—parking, food and beverage concessions, everything. My wife and I sold our home in Michigan and purchased a new house in Houston, where we resolved to live for several years until my assignment was completed.

Now you may be thinking: How in the world did Ford Motor Credit Company ever get into the baseball business? This is, indeed, a fair and logical question, since our principal business is the financing of automobiles.

Well, back in the early 1970s, Ford Credit was in the commercial lending business, and ended up owning a company called the Houston Sports Association. HSA not only owned the Astros baseball team but was the primary lessee of the Astrodome.

A few sports trivia buffs know that "Judge" Roy Hofheinz was the genius behind the creation of the first domed stadium in the world. While visiting the Roman Colosseum in the 1950s,

Hofheinz came up with the idea of building the Houston Astrodome. Not a wealthy man and lacking the resources to do it himself, Hofheinz, a super pitchman, formed HSA, bringing in some influential partners to participate in the deal. Next, Harris County, where the Dome is located, issued bonds to raise the necessary funds. Construction began in 1962 and was completed two years later. In the process, HSA secured a 99-year lease with the county for the famed sports arena.

Interestingly, the first home run in the Astrodome was hit, not by a National League player, but by the Yankees' Mickey Mantle. His homer occurred during the first baseball game held in the Dome, an exhibition game between the New York Yankees and the Houston Astros. I can't remember who won.

Unfortunately, a series of events created hard times for HSA. For starters, back then Texas was pure football country, and Texans were not supportive of their newly formed and struggling baseball team. An oil town, Houston was then in the midst of a severe recession resulting from the first OPEC oil crisis, which occurred in 1972. The high cost of oil generated spiraling inflation and very high (by 1970s standards) interest rates. To make matters worse, the Judge didn't get along with his partners, and over a period of time, he kept buying them out. In due time, he owned the whole shooting match, a feat he accomplished by borrowing more and more money. With skyrocketing interest rates, the inevitable happened: Hofheinz had trouble servicing his debt.

Ford Credit and General Electric Credit (which is now General Electric Capital) joined forces on a 50-50 basis, consolidated Hofheinz's debts, and finally, to avoid foreclosure, took over his ownership. This is why, for a couple of years, GE Credit and Ford Credit were partners in a baseball venture that neither company wanted to be in. Although Ford had a close relationship with GE, the management of both companies had different ideas on finding a solution to their mutual problem—how to get out of the baseball business.

Dual ownership made it difficult to move forward, so it was

agreed that only one company should be the sole owner. This way, it would have the freedom to make its own decisions. As a consequence, in 1978, Ford Credit ended up owning HSA. This is when I was dispatched to Houston. My job description was clearly defined. I was to sell the entire baseball package. Everything! The company didn't want to sell it piecemeal—we wanted a clean deal: One buyer would buy everything.

Obviously, I was taking a major career risk. After all, I'd be out of the mainstream of our business. As the saying goes, "Out of sight, out of mind." I had no idea how long my family would be living in Houston. Two to three years was the estimate, but I was hoping to be back in Dearborn even sooner. Still, who could predict? After all, as a manager for a car credit company, I was definitely sailing on uncharted waters.

I arrived in Houston on December 4 to spend a few days getting acquainted with what Ford Credit actually owned and what I'd have to do to sell our holdings. I was surprised to learn that Ford Credit couldn't sell the team to just anyone. Our lease on the Astrodome was with Harris County, which had a landlord's right to refuse to transfer the lease—meaning we needed the county's approval or we couldn't make the sale!

As you can see, it was crucial that we remain on good terms with the half-dozen or so members of the county government who were the decision makers. This wouldn't have been a problem, except for one thing. In March 1979—just two days before the opening of the baseball season—a decision made in Dearborn threatened to make me a very unpopular guy in the Harris County building in downtown Houston. To backtrack, from the very first day the Astros played baseball in the Astrodome—every season from 1964 through 1978—Judge Hofheinz had provided, gratis, a comfortable 162-seat section on the club level for the exclusive use of county employees.

Although it was perfectly all right for the judge as a private citizen to do what he pleased with his baseball team, Ford Credit did not think it appropriate for a publicly owned corporation to, in effect, give something free to government officials. So I had the extremely unpleasant task of going to the county building to inform each administrator, face to face, that there would be no more free season baseball passes. Needless to say, it was probably the toughest day of my career!

One of my first stops was to see Commissioner Farentino. After I explained that there would be no more free tickets and free parking, he informed me in a soft Southern drawl: "That's fine, Bill. You're doing the right thing. I'm glad to see Ford is acting responsibly."

I thanked him for his understanding.

"Just one thing," he added. "Be careful of our speed limits when you're driving in Harris County."

Another person I had to meet with was Commissioner Squatty Lyons (I don't remember his real first name). His secretary wasn't as subtle when she told me, "Commissioner Lyons knows why you're here, and he doesn't want to see you!"

I made still one more visit to Commissioner Jon Lindsey (actually Judge Lindsey), head of the county commissioners, to break the news to him that Ford was no longer able to continue the tradition with the baseball passes. Lindsey accepted it in a gracious manner. But, overall, I felt like I'd been through the wringer that afternoon. Needless to say, it was a long time before I felt at ease when I visited the Harris County building.

Another person I met was John McMullen, a strong-willed, and wealthy, self-made man from New Jersey. McMullen had many business interests—including being a major stockholder of American Shipbuilding—and at one time he owned more stock in the company than even George Steinbrenner. He also owned a piece of the New York Yankees. McMullen's the fellow who caused a big media sensation when he was quoted as saying in reference to Steinbrenner: "There is nothing more limited than a limited partner in the New York Yankees."

That April, I met several times with McMullen, and by May he expressed interest in buying all our baseball holdings in Houston. However, there was just one major obstacle. The

Harris County government officials had said right from the beginning: DON'T SELL THE HOUSTON BASEBALL TEAM TO A DAMN YANKEE.

So I was faced with a real dilemma. I had found not only the best potential buyer, but perhaps the *only* potential buyer. But, no denying it, McMullen was a Yankee. He was born, raised, and living in New Jersey; his offices were in the World Trade Center in New York City. If we could make a deal with him, we could come out whole. Otherwise, it looked like Ford Credit would be in the baseball business for a very, very long time. Although I had found a buyer for the Astros, the *real* sale was the one I'd have to make in convincing the county officials to approve McMullen, a Yankee, as the new owner.

I struggled with finding a solution for many days and an equal amount of sleepless nights. Suddenly, it occurred to me that the seed for selling the county on approving its new Yankee owner had been planted two days before the opening of the 1979 baseball season. The key to winning over the county officials was to demonstrate that having the ownership of the baseball team restored to a private entrepreneur served their best interests. Above all else, it would reestablish some of the privileges they'd become used to—namely, those cherished season baseball passes.

To appease the county officials, McMullen agreed to bring in some Houston partners—A. J. Foyt, the Indy race car driver, was one of them. Having a well-known sports personality and a few other local businesspeople as owners generated a lot of support from the public as well as from the local politicians.

With the approval of the county, in July we began negotiating a contract for McMullen's group to buy our entire baseball interest, and we closed the deal in early September. All in all, it took 10 months to wrap up what had been estimated as a minimum two- to three-year project. My family stayed in Houston for the rest of the month while I made sure the transition of ownership went smoothly. I was back in Dearborn working at my new assignment on October 1, 1979.

Bill Odom illustrates how a large multi-million dollar sales transaction can be made or fall apart all because of a seemingly trite consideration. Odom's resourcefulness stemmed from the fact that he was able to identify definite advantages to Harris County of having a private individual, rather than Ford Credit, a publicly-owned company, as owner of the Houston Astros and lessee of the Astrodome.

Great salesmanship depends on the ability to put yourself in the shoes of your buyer and understand what motivates that individual. It doesn't matter what you are selling or who your buyer is—a consumer of modest means or a giant corporation. The same principle applies. You must be observant to tailor your sales presentation to the needs of your customer.

William E. Odom returned to Ford's world headquarters in Dearborn, and after a series of promotions by Ford Motor Credit Company, was named chairman of the board, a position which he currently holds.

NO GRIEF

Told by Robert L. Shook

A few years ago, I visited the headquarters of one of the world's largest corporations. My meeting followed a lengthy series of correspondence and telephone conversations with John Carson, the company's vice president of public affairs. (Since the nature of this story requires confidentiality, I will refer to the company as the Great American Company. The names of the executives are also fictitious.)

My purpose for scheduling the meeting was to make a presentation to a committee of top executives in order to be granted permission to write a book about the company. Because I wanted to interview approximately 150 company employees, management's sanction was necessary. Without this consent, I didn't think it possible to write the kind of book I was proposing.

I arrived at John Carson's office several minutes before the meeting was to begin. After we exchanged greetings, he said, "Bob, I want you to know I am personally in favor of your writing the book. I think it will be good PR for the company."

"Thank you, John. That's good news," I replied. "What's more, I concur. It will create enormous goodwill for Great American."

"Bob, I want you to know I have recommended it to the members of the committee. But unless you get their approval, it's no done deal."

"The book is such a wonderful thing for this company," I said, "I feel comfortable they will approve it."

"Unfortunately, Bob, I don't share your confidence," Carson said.

"You don't?" I asked.

"Let me start with who will be attending the meeting with us," Carson said. "In addition to Anthony Marks, our CEO, Phil Clinton, our senior vice president of marketing, will attend. And so will Al Rohr, executive vice president of human relations, and Betty Green, the corporate affairs vice president, who will work directly with you if the project is approved.

"Now, the problem is," Carson went on, "everyone will be cordial and agree that your book is a good idea, but no decision will be made on it today. Then, like a helluva lot of other good ideas, it will be buried somewhere. It won't be considered a top company priority, so we'll just never get around to it again. What I'm saying, Bob, is that even though your book has merit, unless it's approved today, it will be indefinitely shelved. With so many things going on around here, in all likelihood it will never be discussed again."

"That's good information for me to know before walking into the lion's den," I said with a faint smile.

"One more thing, Bob," Carson added. "Our meeting is scheduled for 10:30, and Marks has a meeting at 11:00. He can't be late for it, so you have approximately 25 minutes to sell your book."

The meeting was conducted in a beautiful conference room with Anthony Marks at the head of the table. I sensed that if I sold just him, the others would go along with his decision. I knew, however, that I had to sell him today. There would be no second chance.

Carson started the meeting by introducing me, mentioning a few of the titles of other books I had written. He was kind enough to say that he personally enjoyed reading a few I had sent to him. Then he turned to me and said, "Bob, the floor is all yours."

I stood up and said in my most humble and sincere voice: "Ladies and gentlemen, it is indeed an honor and a privilege for me to be here today and address the top-ranking managers who run this great company, truly one of the finest organizations in the history of our nation. Ever since I was a boy, I have been an admirer of Great American."

I knew that what I said sounded mushy, but it was working so I continued: "Addressing the group gathered here today is certainly a major highlight in my career. After all, you are responsible for the future of this international multi-billion dollar corporation, which is an awesome responsibility. Now you're giving your valuable time to me so I can tell you about a book I want to write about the history of Great American and how it is professionally managed today."

I had laid it on really thick, and I continued: "With all the important decisions you people have to make to operate this company, approving my book has to be one of the really easy and minor ones that comes your way. In fact, in comparison to some of the really big decisions, this one must be a piece of cake for you to make.

"I'm so delighted that you invited me to this meeting today, because I know that 20 minutes from now when I walk out of here, I'll know exactly what your decision is. And that's what I admire about top executives with successful, well-managed corporations in the same league as Great Western. I won't mention names," I continued in a lowered voice, "but I once met with another large corporation, and you couldn't begin to believe how much grief I had to endure because of its inability to make decisions. Everything had to go through some immense bureaucratic shuffle before anything could get done. Well, I vowed that never again would I subject myself to working with a corporation so bogged down in bureaucracy that its top management can't make important decisions. I have enough good book ideas to write that I don't need that kind of grief in my life. I am at a stage in my career that if I even sense a company is going to put me through such grief, I'll simply walk away and work with another company."

Then, without missing a beat, I went on to give a 10-minute chapter-by-chapter presentation of what I intended to write about the company. Then I conducted a 5-minute question-and-answer session.

After I answered a few questions, Marks said, "I see no reason why we can't give Mr. Shook the go-ahead so he can get started with his book. Does anyone disagree?"

Everyone nodded in approval, and Marks excused himself so he could rush to his next meeting. Carson took over and thanked everyone for attending. "Bob and Betty," he said, "I'd like to go over a few things with you in my office."

Behind his closed door, Carson told me, "I would have never believed it if I didn't see it with my own eyes. I didn't think your book had a snowball's chance in hell of being approved at the meeting. I congratulate you on one great selling job."

I closed the sale with my opening remarks. Frequently, it's what you say in the beginning of a sales presentation or in its middle that actually closes the sale. Contrary to common belief, the close is not necessarily at the end of the sale. Notice how this close worked on a group of some of the nation's most high-powered executives—the same close I used to sell many small business owners during my life insurance career. I would simply say, "What I enjoy so much about working with entrepreneurs such as you, sir, is that you're capable of making a decision on the spot. This is the difference between a person who is in business for himself and a worker who is employed by somebody else."

After you flatter people on their ability to be decisive, they don't want to procrastinate or give the impression that they are unable to make a buying decision. When you play up to people's ego by confirming that they are decisive, they don't want to deflate your expectations by not being able to make a decision. This selling technique can be used with practically anybody.

PERSEVERANCE PAYS OFF

Told by Ross Perot

In August 1957, upon completing my four-year term of duty in the Navy, I joined IBM as a sales trainee. With a starting pay of $500 a month, I began the company's data processing sales training program. After 18 months, I was ready to hit the pavement as an IBM salesman. Having a young family, I was chomping at the bit to start selling so I could make some commissions.

A prime prospect in my territory was Southwestern Life Insurance Company, which had been called on by many IBM salespeople prior to my coming aboard, but to no avail. In fact, IBMers had called on Southwestern so many times that a directive was sent to the front doorman that no IBM salespeople were even allowed to enter the building. Knowing this made me all the more determined to sell our data processing service. After several attempts to get past the doorman, I was finally able to get my foot in the door. I suppose the doorman just got tired of saying no to me. Over a period of time, I met with the company's top managers and eventually had them all sold on IBM—that is, with one exception: Ralph Wood, the chairman of the board.

The stalemate presented a problem, because Wood refused to see me. I knew that if I was ever going to make the sale, he was the guy I had to win over. Without his approval, there wouldn't be a sale!

I started to think of ways to meet with him, and then I remembered something that was mentioned in our training class. We were told that the IBM company always stood behind its sales reps. If any of us ever needed a scientific person, a technician, a senior officer—whomever—the company would fly that person in from New York, California, from anywhere. IBM really emphasized its strong backup team. Well, with the stalemate I ran into at Southwestern, I went directly to Henry Wendler, the Dallas district sales manager, and said, "I'd like to have Tom Watson [the CEO and son of IBM's founder, Thomas Watson, Sr.] come down here to make a call with me to meet the chairman."

"Why do you need him?" Wendler asked.

"I want Ralph Wood to hear from Watson what we are doing in other places with other insurance firms and how we can do it for Southwestern," I said.

Asking for our CEO to make a call with a new sales rep must have caught Wendler off guard. "Mr. Watson is a great guy and a wonderful salesman," he replied, "but he isn't an expert on insurance. How about if we bring in Gil Jones, the president of data processing? I know Jones has worked with several major insurers in Newark, New Jersey, where he once was manager. Let's ask him to come down."

That sounded fine with me. Wendler called Jones, who agreed to swing by Dallas the following Friday after attending a meeting in Florida. Then I called Wood, and told him the president of IBM's data processing division was in town and wanted to meet with him. Wood finally agreed to see me.

Having Henry Wendler and Gil Jones accompany me was a real confidence builder. Additionally, in preparation for the meeting, I stayed up late for several nights reading everything I could about Southwestern and the insurance industry. Being fully prepared also served as a confidence booster to me. When the three of us entered Wood's office, I'll never forget the greeting he gave us: "I was supposed to be hunting quail today so I hope you have something important to say."

Although Wood listened to our presentation, I sensed we weren't making any headway with him. As we were about to leave his office, I put in my final two cents: "Mr. Wood, one reason I asked my two bosses to come here today to meet you is that I wanted them to hear me tell you that I would be available full time to serve Southwestern. The company will back me 100 percent and I'll get whatever help that's required from our special representatives and support teams. That's so we can make Southwestern one of IBM's most outstanding installations in the country."

My comment didn't seem to faze Wood, and after we walked out, Jones' only words to me were: "Ross, get another prospect."

However, on Monday morning, Wood called down to one of his vice presidents and said, "Who was that kid in here with Jones? Is he an actuary or something?"

Well, Gil Jones got me in, but I got to make my sales presentation. And I do not happen to be an actuary. But evidently all the studying I did on the life insurance industry and boning up on Southwestern must have made an impression on him. A few weeks later, Wood agreed to meet with me, and this time I asked him a lot of questions in order to figure out how our machines could solve his problems. Back in those days, IBM mostly rented its machines, but customers also could purchase the equipment. When I found out Southwestern's workload would keep a machine busy for only one shift, I was able to convince Wood to buy the equipment and rent time to Blue Cross to use during the night shift. This way, by sharing the cost, Southwestern and Blue Cross both came out ahead.

Six weeks from the date I first got in to see Mr. Wood, I presented him with a contract, and a few days after he had time to review it, we met again to get the order signed.

Instead I was greeted with: "There's one thing in the contract I want changed before I sign it."

"What's that?" I asked.

"It won't do any good to tell you because you won't be able to get it done."

He had good reason to say that. Back in those days, IBM would never change a contract. Still, I said, "Go ahead, tell me." He did and it really wasn't anything significant. In fact, it was so insignificant, I can't even recall what it was.

"Well, if this is what you want," I said, "I will try to do it for you."

Later that afternoon, I called the head of IBM's legal department. It was a call I will never forget. I told him, "You can help me make the largest sale ever made in this part of the country. All we have to do is make a minor change to the contract."

"Ross, we normally don't change the contract."

"I don't think this is important," I replied.

"What change do you want?" he asked.

After I explained it to him, there were a few moments of silence, and he said, "We'll do it."

"Send me a wire," I said, "And I'll take it to Mr. Wood at Southwestern tomorrow morning."

I took the wire to Wood's office, and I told him we would make the change in the contract he requested. I handed him the wire. As he read it, I laid the contract down on his desk and handed him a pen.

"Perot, you tricked me," he said, throwing the pen down on his desk. Then he grinned and signed the contract.

The deal turned out to be a highly successful contract for IBM, and Southwestern was very pleased with its computer system. Wood was a tough old guy, and I thought the world of him. Years later, after I started EDS whenever I'd see him, he'd always give me a warm greeting and jokingly say, "Perot, have you gone broke yet?"

Ross Perot's perseverance paid off, and in time he became one of the greatest sales reps in IBM history. Persistence is a trait for which he became renowned, and a significant factor in his enormous success. After leaving IBM and starting EDS, Perot says his company once conducted a study showing that 85 percent of its customer base had said no at least once before buying. "I used to love to tell our people this," he says, "because if you have a good idea, you have to keep going back and keep marketing it—you've got to keep calling on the prospects."

Ross Perot worked for IBM for five years before he left to start Electronic Data Systems (EDS) in Dallas in 1962. In 1984, EDS was sold to General Motors for $2.5 billion. Later he formed Perot Systems, Inc., a computer systems company also based in Dallas. In 1992, Perot ran for President of the United States against George Bush and Bill Clinton.

DO OR DIE

Told by F. Pete Gulick

I was only 25 years old when I joined Casekraft Corporation, a small supplier of retail store fixture displays in Manchester, Kentucky. I was brought in as vice president of marketing; my job was to generate some large national accounts. At the time, Casekraft's annual revenues were under $1 million, and the goal was to boost sales into the $5 to $7 million range.

One national retailer on my "hit list" was Federated Department Stores, which is headquartered in Cincinnati, Ohio, about three hours by car from Manchester. In the beginning, I bombarded the retail chain with mailings, telephone calls, and personal visits. My objective was for our company to become qualified to make a bid for some of Federated's fixture display business. My main hurdle was the fact that Federated's management had never heard of us. Plus, management was concerned about us being so small that we didn't have the capacity to handle a big job. In time, however, my persistence paid off. Eventually, we were allowed to submit a bid package for a Lazarus department store remodeling job in Louisville, Kentucky. The job involved remodeling the cosmetics and women's clothing department on the first floor. The project was perhaps small potatoes to Federated, but at $750,000 it was big time to us!

Our bid was received and reviewed. Our pricing was considered competitive. This meant we would go to Federated's Cincinnati corporate offices to make a formal presentation to an executive vice president and an assistant vice president.

The big day to meet with them soon arrived. In the elevator, I remember saying aloud to myself: "Life all comes down to a few moments and this is one of them." I always give myself this same pep talk before an important sales presentation. It gives me that extra shot of adrenaline. Our president and general manager were accompanying me on this important sales call. "What did you say?" the president asked.

What I said to myself was not meant for anyone to hear, but I answered, "Life all comes down to a few moments and this is one of them." The two men smiled at me as we stepped off the elevator onto the plush carpeting of the executive suite floor. I smiled back, knowing my comment pumped them up too.

We had done our homework well, and we entered a boardroom with full confidence. We made a beautiful sales presentation, covering all the details, including the minute points of the contract. Several times during the course of the meeting I asked for the order, and each time there was no assurance we would get the job. One constant rebuttal was: "Casekraft is such a small company, and you have never done a job this size. Frankly, we are concerned about whether you have the resources to handle it. Considering your track record, there is no indication you can do what you say you'll do."

"Because we are small," I retorted, "we are light on our feet. We can move on a dime. We're at your call, around the clock, 24 hours a day, 365 days a year. If you need to contact any of us, you can deal directly with any one of us at any time—the president, the general manager and the vice president of marketing. With a big firm, you'd be working with somebody further down the chain of command. With us, you are by far our most important customer. Yes, sir, our size is an advantage to you."

Though I presented every reason that being small was not a disadvantage but an advantage, he refused to make a commitment. I knew that if we left his office without a signed order, chances were slim that we would get the job.

The executive vice president concluded the meeting by saying, "Thank you very much for your time, gentlemen. We will study your proposal and get back with you."

The three of us stood up, briefcases in hand, and began saying our good-byes. I sensed the Federated vice presidents were convinced that our sales presentation was over. They became more relaxed, as if they were thinking, "The heat is off. Pete is backing off; he will go away and let us make our decision when we feel like it."

As we shook hands and were heading toward the door, I sensed that the timing was right and added, "Oh, just one more thing that I want to bring to your attention."

Caught off guard, the department store vice president said, "Sure, Pete, what?"

"There is one very important issue I haven't mentioned. Do you realize what's at stake here for Casekraft?"

He looked at me with a puzzled expression on his face.

"To us, we are putting our future on the line. That's right. Our company's future is at stake, gentlemen. If we don't perform in accordance with this contract, our reputation for doing big jobs is ruined. Just imagine what will happen if the word were to spread that we failed to live up to Federated's expectations. Sir, we are staking our future on this job. Believe me, we would not take such a risk if we were not fully confident that we could do the job."

There was a brief pause, and the executive vice president replied, "Pete, you just made an excellent point." Again there was silence.

"Let me take this proposal and run it by our accounting department. By the time you get back to your office in Manchester, I will have faxed a signed purchase order to you."

When we returned to our plant, there was the order that doubled the size of Casekraft's revenues for the previous year.

A resourceful salesperson understands that timing is essential. Even after it appears that the sales presentation is over, the salesperson can present a forceful reason that his or her company should be awarded an order. Pete did this brilliantly. And in the process, he doubled his company's revenues with a single sale!

In early 1994, F. Pete Gulick joined Ontario Store Fixtures, Inc., a Toronto-based manufacturer of retail store fixtures and displays, as director of sales. OSFI is the largest company in its field in North America.

HAVING A
CLEAR OBJECTIVE

Told by Zig Ziglar

This is a story about how my wife, Jean, sold me on buying a home that was more than I thought I could afford at the time. It is my favorite sales story—even though I was the one who got sold!

When we first moved to Dallas in 1968 we were temporarily living in a motel. I was teaching a class in sales and motivation from 9 a.m. to 9 p.m. six days a week while Jean worked with real estate brokers looking for a place for us to live. After considerable discussion, we had agreed to a "reasonable" figure to invest in our new home.

After we arrived at an exact amount, she asked, "Honey, if we were to find our *dream* house, how much *more* can we invest?"

While $20,000 doesn't seem like a lot of money today, it was back then, and after a long discussion, this is the amount we agreed upon—over and beyond our fixed amount.

Once this was settled, she sat me on the edge of the bed in our motel room and began describing her "find."

"Honey, I found our dream home. It's absolutely gorgeous! Four beautiful bedrooms on a big lot, plenty of room in the backyard for you to build that arrow-shaped swimming pool you've been talking about, walk-in closets in every room, and four bathrooms!"

"How much does that house cost?" I interrupted.

"Honey, you'll have to see it to believe it, but you're going to love it because the den is monstrous and it has exposed beams and a cathedral ceiling. The garage is so big we will have room for the two cars and all our tools. Best of all, honey, there's an 11' × 11' spot for you to build that little office where you can do the writing you've been talking about. And, honey, the master bedroom is so big we're going to have to get a riding vacuum cleaner!"

"But, sweetheart," I interrupted again, "How much..."

She told me it was $18,000—more—than the *maximum*, which was already $20,000 more than what I thought we could afford to spend.

After some more discussion, I agreed to take a look at it and meet with the builder—but on the condition that I was only looking. The next evening, after we pulled into the driveway and walked in the front door, I knew I was in big trouble. The house was beautiful and I instantly wanted it—but there is a world of difference between what we want and what we sometimes get.

This is when I started treating the builder the same way I've been treated by prospects whom I called on all during my sales career. Even though I was interested and truly *excited*, I acted nonchalant, as if I didn't care one way or another if we bought it. That's right. I was scared to show an interest because I knew that any slight hint I gave would make it that much harder for me to say no to my wife and the builder.

I agreed to see the house "as long as we were there." and Jean took me first to the den and, with bubbling enthusiasm, she said, "Look at the size of this den, honey, and aren't those exposed beams gorgeous?"

Without waiting for an answer, she continued, "And just look at *your* fireplace with all those bookshelves around it for *your* books. I just can't wait to see you watching the Cowboys whip up on somebody on Sunday afternoon out of one eye and watching *your* fire out of the other one."

In the master bedroom, she didn't lose one iota of her enthusiasm. "Just look at the size of this room, honey. There's plenty of room for the king-size bed and we could put our two chairs and table over here. It's perfect for us, because you know how we like to get up in the morning and have our coffee and quiet time together. And, honey, just look at *your* closet. Why, even as messy as you are, there's plenty of room for everything."

Still on a nonstop basis, she led me to the door going to the backyard. "Plenty of room for *your* arrow-shaped swimming pool. We can put the point of the arrow in the direction of the garage, and the diving board on the other end will still be 10 feet from the neighbor's lot."

In the garage, she said, "Plenty of room for two cars, and here's that 11' × 11' space for you to build *your* office you've planned for so long."

Once inside the house again, she said, "This bedroom is for Susie, and when she's gone from home in a couple of years, we'll have that guest bedroom we've always wanted."

When the tour was finally over, she squeezed my hand and asked, "How do you feel about it, honey?"

Obviously, she knew the answer before she asked the question. She knew I loved it, and for me to say anything different would be untrue. "It's a beautiful home, but you know perfectly well that we can't afford a house like this," I told her.

She dropped the subject, and it wasn't until the next morning that she asked, "Honey, how long do you think we'll be living in Dallas?"

"Mmm, 30 years," I said, figuring that my life expectancy was at least that given my age of 40 at the time.

"How much does that $18,000 figure out per year?" she asked.

"Well, $18,000 for 30 years would be $600 a year," I quickly calculated, as if she hadn't already known the exact amount.

"How much is that a month?" she continued.

"That would be $50 a month."

"How much is that a day?"

"Now, honey, your math is as good as mine. It comes to about $1.70 a day, but why do you ask all these questions?" I said.

"Honey, could I ask you one more question?"

I knew I was in the process of being had, but I said, "Why, sure."

"Honey, would you give another $1.70 a day to have a *happy* wife—instead of just a wife?"

Need I continue? You know where we live today.

There are many lessons to be learned from the way my wife sold me. First, like any good salesperson, she refused to listen to any negative objections that I voiced when I said we couldn't afford it. Too many salespeople stop right there when it would be wise for them to be a *little hard of hearing!* To her credit, Jean did it so smoothly because she never became defensive, argumentative, or antagonistic. Throughout her entire presentation, she was lovingly and enthusiastically optimistic that she was going to make the sale. Nor did she argue when I talked about not being able to afford it— another thing that salespeople tend to do to their detriment.

What I think was best about her presentation was that she clearly understood that she needed to make only an $18,000 sale. Prior to going house hunting, she knew that she had already "sold" the price we could pay. She had even "sold" the idea of paying an extra $20,000. Like every super salesperson, she understood that there was no need to discuss what had already been decided.

Likewise, if a prospect tells you he's willing to spend $200,000, and your product costs $230,000, you have to sell him only on the $30,000 additional cost. It is essential for you to realize that you do not have to sell something worth $230,000— only $30,000 worth of additional value, to justify what the prospect is willing to spend.

As Zig explains, there are several lessons to be learned from his wife's presentation. In particular, I like the way she closed the sale when she broke the $18,000 down to only $1.70—a very small price for any man to pay to make his spouse happy. By the way, is it interesting to see how Zig tried to pretend he wasn't excited about the house, even though he was? There's a good lesson here too. Your customers don't always want you to know how they really feel about your product—when they do want to buy it!

Zig Ziglar is considered America's number-one sales motivator. A resident of Dallas, Texas, Zig has written 10 books, including two best-sellers on sales: Secrets of Closing the Sale *and* Ziglar on Selling. *His book* See You at the Top, *the eighth best-selling hardcover book of the last decade, still sells roughly 50,000 copies each year. Early in his career, he was the number-one cookware salesman in America for Saladmaster Corporation, headquartered in Dallas.*

BEING AN "IMPARTIAL" THIRD PARTY

Told by Robert L. Shook

W hen I was doing research for my book *Turnaround: The New Ford Motor Company,* I interviewed several suppliers of automobile parts for Ford. My research put me in contact with owners and CEOs of small manufacturing companies that employed 500 to 2000 workers.

One of my good friends and business associates, Ari Deshe, president of Employee Benefits Systems, Inc. (EBS), came to me with a wonderful idea. Ari explained that his agency specialized in selling payroll deduction life insurance policies, and he believed these companies were ideal prospects. "The hardest part about selling a payroll deduction plan," he said, "is getting in to see the decision maker. Bob, if you could introduce me to some of your contacts, I will compensate you with a large fee that will make it worth your while." Ari estimated that some fees would be as high as $50,000. For fees in these amounts, I agreed not only to set up appointments but to accompany him to make personal introductions.

We set up an appointment to see Phil Baylor, owner and CEO of Baylor Plastics (this is a fictitious company but all the facts are true), a company that had 1500 employees. We then made a personal call. In other words, Baylor knew what we were coming to see him for, and he agreed to hear Ari out. I made the introduction in the following manner: "Ari is the president of EBS, a company that specializes in providing fringe benefits to company employees, and there is no cost to the employer. Basically, EBS offers life insurance benefits that are sold on an individual basis but at group rates. Physical examinations are not required, and regardless of health every employee is eligible to participate. Phil, all you have to do is permit EBS to send one premium billing to the company each month, deduct the premiums from those employees who enroll in the program, and send one monthly check to EBS. Ari is one of the foremost experts in the country in his field. He is a man of the upmost integrity, and I know you will enjoy doing business with him."

They shook hands and I said, "Now that I've introduced the two of you, I'm going to keep quiet and let Ari do all the talking. After all, he's the expert."

We sat down at Baylor's desk, and Ari began his detailed presentation. His expertise was clearly evident. For nearly two hours, he fielded every question, and when he was through, Baylor knew everything he needed to know about the plan.

"It's something we should definitely do for our employees," Baylor said.

"Is there anything I can tell you that isn't perfectly clear?" Ari asked.

"No, you did an excellent job, Ari. And Bob, I want to thank you for introducing me to Ari," Baylor replied. Turning to Ari, he added, "I'm sure we'll do business. How about if I get back to you in a week or two?"

Ari consented, and packed up his briefcase. The three of us shook hands and said our good-byes. Baylor started walking us toward the door of his office.

"Hey, wait just one minute," I exclaimed. "I'm having a problem here."

Phil and Ari froze in their tracks. Neither said a word, and I continued. "Let's sit down for a moment. There is something I have to ask both of you," I said. Without waiting for a response, I seated myself at the desk. They followed my lead and joined me.

"You both know that I am an author, and I've written several books on selling. I'm presently working on a manuscript titled *Hardball: How to Turn the Pressure on Without Turning the Customer Off*, and I've been doing a lot of research on it. Now, in some circles, I'm considered somewhat of an expert on the subject of selling, and I've just witnessed something today that has me completely mystified."

The surprised looks on their faces were still there, and turning to Baylor, I continued, "Phil, you agree that Ari did an excellent job in the manner which he explained his proposal to you, don't you?"

"Yes, I agree. He did an outstanding job."

"And, now," I added, "and correct me if I'm wrong, I assume that you are interested in what he has to offer."

"That's a correct assumption, Bob."

I then turned to Ari and said, "Now, and you correct me if I'm wrong, I also assume that you want Baylor Plastics as a client."

"Absolutely," he answered (as if I didn't know).

"If I may continue, gentlemen," I said, "as a third party witnessing a sales presentation, I observe one party who wants to buy (I pointed to Baylor) and another who wants to sell (I turned my head toward Ari). This being the case, I don't see any reason in the world that Ari should make a special trip back here to have you, Phil, put your John Hancock on a piece of paper so he can start the ball rolling and begin your enrollment. The way I see things, that would be an inefficient use of time."

Before Baylor could say a word, I added, "Ari, would you *please*—and if for no other reason, do it for my sake—have Phil sign an application."

Ari picked up my cue and placed the papers on desk. "I need your okay on this line and on this one right here," he said. Without the slightest hesitation, Baylor signed his name.

This sale resulted in a six-figure commission, and I firmly believe that it might have fallen through if I had not "assisted" with its close. Incidentally, Ari had initially tipped me off that his closing ratio was miniscule on callbacks. He explained that although everybody always agreed on the merit of his plan, if a buying decision was postponed, the prospect gave it little priority afterward. Then, as time elapsed, the prospect thought less and less about the need to implement a payroll deduction plan, and eventually cooled off about it.

Although I put on my author's hat, this technique can be effectively executed by a sales manager who is accompanying one of his or her salespeople. In this scenario, the sales manager would preface his or her remarks by saying, "As John's sales manager"—district sales supervisor, the company's vice president of marketing, and so on—"I'd like to make a comment."

EIGHT

SERVICING THE CUSTOMER

Early on in my career, I once heard a salesman remark, "The sale doesn't begin until *after* the sale." Back then, I didn't understand what he was saying.

Years later, I understood exactly what he meant. The two words *sell* and *service* must always go together. You can't separate them, because you can't have one without the other. Real success in the sales field comes only from repeat orders and referrals from satisfied customers. In today's highly competitive marketplace, I truly don't think it is possible to succeed in even a modest way without providing excellent service to your customers.

In this final part of the book, you will discover how outstanding service pays off in big dividends—how servicing the customer is what ultimately determines success in the sales field. Each of these stories reiterates this message.

FROM TINY ACORNS GROW MIGHTY OAKS

Told by Richard Luisi

O ne day when I was out canvassing, I called on a woman who owned three Electrolux machines.

"I'm a big fan of Electrolux," she said. "I keep one upstairs and another downstairs, and I also have one of your shampoo-polishers."

She explained that after the representative sold her the machines, he had never come around again. This was contrary to my sales philosophy, because I believed in keeping in touch with my customers. It was my practice to do four things whenever I'd be in a customer's home:

1. Always show something new.
2. Leave my name and number by putting stickers on the equipment and in the customer's personal phone book.
3. Get three referrals.
4. Stay in touch every four months.

"As long as I'm here," I said, "let me take a look at your machines."

She invited me in and I took apart the power nozzles and cleaned them for her. I also put my stickers on her machines and said, "If you ever have any problems or need any supplies, ma'am, be sure to call me." She was very grateful.

Then out of habit, I said, "While I'm here, let me show you our new shampooer and our new vacuum." Although I didn't expect to sell her anything, I went over the new products, feature by feature. (I believe in the law of averages.)

"Gosh, I like them," she said. "Can I trade my old ones in?"

I ended up selling her two machines on a trade-in basis, and she referred me to three neighbors and three relatives, all of whom bought. She was very active in her church and gave me a list of people there. As a consequence of knocking on that one door, during the next six months I sold 50 additional machines.

Everybody loves service. Although good service should be standard operating procedure, so few salespeople give it, that customers are surprised when they do. As a consequence, customers value outstanding service and are delighted to refer their friends and relatives to salespeople who excel at it.

Richard Luisi is an area vice president for Electrolux. (Read more about him in "It Pays to Advertise" in Part Four.)

FULL-SERVICE REAL ESTATE SELLING

Told by Cindy Rossmeisl

I recently closed a land deal with Wal-Mart in Sparta, New Jersey, for $2.6 million. It was one of the easiest sales I ever made. An out-of-town broker walked into my office one day and said: "I know you're in residential sales, but would you work with me on a commercial property?"

"Sure. But why did you come to me?" I asked.

"When I first got into Sparta, I stopped by the service station and asked the owner if he knew any good real estate brokers in town. He recommended you. Then I asked the same question to the guy who owns the diner, and again you were the first choice. I made one more stop at the supermarket, and for the third straight time you were named. I heard all I need to know. Now this is my fourth stop. I'm looking for a lot to build a Wal-Mart on. Will you help me find one?"

I was flattered to come so highly recommended, but nowadays, with my eight years of experience in the business, this sort of thing happens regularly. Of course, it's no accident. I've worked hard to provide my clients with exceptional service, and all the effort I've put into servicing people is beginning to pay off.

I'd have to say Jack Luba, the owner of that service station, is my biggest fan. Whenever somebody asks him for a real estate broker's name, he can't seem to get me fast enough. He even has my beeper number, so if he can't reach me by phone, he beeps me to come right down. This is how I first met Sharon and Bill Hengen. They drove over from Westfield, New Jersey, and while they were buying gas, they happened to mention to Jack that they were looking at lakefronts and were thinking about relocating here. That's all he had to hear. He immediately sent them to my office. Rather than selling them a specific home, however, I took them around the area and sold them on the lifestyle. For example, I told them about our town's annual Fourth of July parade, and how the entire community gets involved. "We have free hot dogs and soda, and in the late afternoon our water-skiing team puts on a show at Lake Mohawk. There's dining on our boardwalk, and that's where I like to watch the fireworks." Then I talked to them about our excellent school system, how Lake Mohawk residents can join its country club—in short, all the wonderful reasons that I sold myself a home in Sparta three months after I started working in the town.

I showed the Hengens some lakefront homes that needed fixing up—which is what Bill said he wanted to do. There was one in particular that they liked in the $350,000 range. As it turned out, they decided it wasn't exactly the type of home they were looking for; besides, it was a little more money than they wanted to spend. "We'll just stay put for the time being," Sharon said.

Although they didn't buy a house, I stayed in constant touch with them, keeping them up to date on what was going on in town. About five months after I first met them, Bill called me and said, "You know, Cindy, all I do is think about the town. What you did was, you sold me the town without selling me a house. We could have found a *house* anywhere, but Sharon and I kept thinking we had to come back and live in Sparta."

They ended up buying a $600,000 home at Sunset Lakes, a brand new, gorgeous community in Sparta located about 2½ miles from Lake Mohawk.

Once I sell a home, my full-service concept begins in earnest. When people are new in the area, I'll line them up with doctors, dentists, lawyers, and cleaning people. And you already know where I send them to buy their gasoline. I'll even help them find a baby-sitter. Before my daughter Sarah went away to college, she would do everything from baby-sitting to keeping my client's teenagers informed of what styles the other kids wore in school. My husband, Phil, and Phil, Jr. pitch in too. Once when a woman's washing machine hose broke, and she couldn't turn it off, my son ran over and fixed it for her. Yeah, I'm usually the first person the new ones call when something goes wrong.

Another time, a woman's alarm system went off one night when her husband was out of town, so she called me to come over while she waited for the police to arrive. I quickly threw some clothes on, jumped in our jeep, and got there before the police. The woman was a nervous wreck, so in order to calm her down, I went through the house to make sure nobody was hiding inside. Thank goodness, nobody was!

My clients are more than clients—many of them have become my good friends. And as a way of expressing my appreciation to them, I throw a big party during the Christmas holidays. My husband is a retired army captain, so we hold the party at the Officers' Club in Dover. I bring in a five- to seven-piece band from New York. There's an open bar, and either filet mignon or chicken française is served. Black tie is optional. Anybody who refers business to me is also invited. One other thing. I always have favors for my guests. At this year's party, I had packets for everyone to pick up at the door on the way home. The packets included a calendar to put on the fridge, a pen with my name on it, and lots of other little items—you know, the kind of stuff that makes people remember me.

With the kind of service that Cindy Rossmeisl provides, it's a sure thing that nobody is going to ever forget her. No wonder she's so successful. Just writing about Cindy makes me want to buy a home from her—the only thing is, living in New Jersey is not particularly convenient for me. Service, service, service. The name of the game is service. Cindy gives her clients so much service that, when it comes to buying a home or referring a real estate person to somebody, they feel guilty even *thinking* about another realtor. This is the way it is with all salespeople who give exceptional service.

Cindy Rossmeisl began her real estate career in 1986 when she joined Weichert Realtors, the largest privately owned real estate brokerage firm in the United States. Among Weichert's more than 8000 salespeople, Cindy ranks as one of the firm's top agents. In 1993, her sales exceeded $10 million. She and her family reside in Sparta, New Jersey, and she works out of the Weichert office in nearby Rockaway.

GOING THAT
EXTRA MILE

Told by Roger Dow

B ack in the summer of 1973, when I was a young, aggressive
sales manager at the Miami Airport Marriott Hotel, I had
heard that the Church of God in Christ, an African-American
religious group, was having a convention in downtown Miami
over the Fourth of July weekend. Although the airport is five
miles away, I hoped I could get some of the church's business.

As you might expect, that particular holiday weekend turns
Miami into a ghost town. The entire city's hotel occupancy was
estimated to run around 3 percent. Unless I drummed up some
business, our hotel could anticipate filling only a handful of
rooms over the holiday weekend.

When I learned that Bishop James was the man in charge of
the convention, I contacted him. "Bishop James," I said, "I don't
think you want your people staying at rundown hotels in downtown Miami. Many of the hotels are closed for the summer, and
even though they will open for the weekend during your group's
stay in town, they'll close down immediately thereafter. You can see
that your people won't get the facilities or service they deserve."

"But your hotel is all the way out at the airport," Bishop
James said.

"That's true, sir. However, because of the holiday there won't be any traffic, so being eight minutes away from the convention center won't be a problem," I assured him. "Having first-class rooms for your people is the important thing you want."

"Thanks for the information," Bishop James replied. "I'll get in touch with you when I'm in town next month."

Bishop James kept his word. The following month, I showed him our facilities. After the grand tour, he said, "You know, we can fill your hotel. If you save us a block of rooms, we'll encourage our people to stay with you."

"That's great," I replied, and I put aside a block of 250 of our 258 rooms for his convention. I knew that, under normal circumstances, I wouldn't sell more than a handful of rooms over the Fourth of July weekend. I wrote up a contract and was very pleased with my newfound business.

A month later, I began to worry. The reservations were not coming in as I had anticipated. I phoned Bishop James and said, "Sir, so far, we have only one room reserved."

"Well, Mr. Dow, what happens," he explained, "is that the downtown hotels will fill up first, and then the people who have waited until the very last minute will come in. Don't worry, Mr. Dow. As the convention approaches, your hotel will fill up."

I felt relieved after talking to him. Our people were getting excited about the convention, and we started putting our staffing levels together to get ready for the Church of God in Christ's guests. In the meantime, I kept reassuring our staff that people were going to show up. By June 20, however, we had only 10 reservations, and I became extraordinarily nervous.

Again I called Bishop James. "You've got to help me, Bishop," I pleaded.

"Trust me," he answered. "I will help you. I know you've worked very hard, Brother Dow"—by now I was Brother Dow—"and I will be sure that we take care of your hotel."

Once more, I felt relieved, but not for long. Three days before the convention, we still had only 10 rooms reserved.

When I found out that Bishop James was in town for a precon-vention meeting, I drove downtown to meet with him.

"I have to see Bishop James," I said to one of his staff.

"You'll have to wait," I was told. "Bishop James is in a meeting." One hour later, I was ushered in to see him.

"Bishop James, I'm in trouble," I said. "You promised me this great business, so I booked it, but nothing has happened yet except for 10 rooms."

"I'll tell you what's happened, Brother Dow," he said. "Our people think your hotel is too far away. If you would rent buses and run transportation back and forth to the convention center, I can still fill your hotel."

I rushed back to my general manager and explained the situation to him. "If we have the buses, we can fill this hotel," I explained.

"Are you sure, Roger?" he questioned. "I don't want to throw good money after bad."

"I believe this will do it," I said.

A commitment was then made to set up hourly transporta-tion to take people back and forth between our hotel and the center, starting the day before the convention. Our buses began going back and forth as planned. Unfortunately, they didn't have any passengers! Only 15 rooms were filled. The night the con-vention kicked off, I rushed down to the Miami convention cen-ter, where there must have been 4000 to 5000 church members in attendance. "I need to see the Bishop," I said desperately to somebody at a registration table.

"You're welcome to go inside and attend our service," she told me sweetly, "and as soon as they take up the collection, you can go up to see the Bishop."

I went into the filled convention hall. Since I was one of the few white people there, it was easy for Bishop James to notice me from the front stage. During the collection, I went on the stage and pulled him aside.

"Bishop," I whispered, "I have a big problem. I have gone on the line for you. I rented buses, and we have only 15 rooms occupied."

"I will take care of it, Brother Dow," he promised. "Now just stand on the side."

Bishop James walked up to the lectern and addressed the audience. "Brothers and sisters, I would like for you to turn your heads to the left. Standing there is Brother Dow, who has been a friend of ours through the entire time we've been in Miami. He is the sales manager of the new Miami Airport Marriott Hotel." All eyes turned toward me and the Bishop continued, "We have committed that we are going to stay at his hotel. Right now he has many open first-class rooms. Is there anyone who is not satisfied with his or her accommodations? If there is, I am telling you to please move out. Brother Dow will provide transportation and rooms for you."

Afterward, dozens of people approached me with complaints. For instance, a mother accompanied by her young children had tears in her eyes as she said, "We were put in a hotel room that hasn't been opened for years. We've got cockroaches in our room!" Beginning at 10 o'clock that night, we started shuttling people back and forth from substandard hotels and rooming houses, and when I finally got to bed at 3 the next morning, we had about 100 rooms rented out. About an hour later, the front desk night auditor called me. "Roger, I know it's late, but I had to call you so you'd get a good night's sleep. I just had the last busload of people show up. It looks like we're going to sell out."

"That's wonderful!" I exclaimed.

By the next morning, the hotel was booked solidly for the next four days.

In this story, a 24-year-old sales manager put everything on the line to get business, and just when he was feeling comfortable, everything seemed to fall apart. But Roger Dow had the tenacity to keep going. Faced with several obstacles, he kept in constant touch with his customer, always communicating problem areas. Undoubtedly, what kept the sale alive was "staying in touch with the customer." In doing so, he built a personal relationship with Bishop James, a man of obvious integrity, who had a sense of fairness and empathy for Dow's predicament. Dow's willingness to do whatever it took truly saved the sale. When the situation looked hopeless, he went that extra mile by spending additional money to provide transportation. As a consequence, what appeared doomed to be a blowout resulted in a highly success-ful sale.

Roger Dow is vice president and general sales manager for Marriott Hotels, Resorts, and Suites. Dow began his career with Marriott in 1966, when he worked as a lifeguard at their sixth hotel. He has since operated in virtually every aspect of sales and marketing. Today, he heads a sales force of 1200 people for the chain's 250 hotels.

THE $10,000 SALE THAT BECAME A $20 MILLION SALE

Told by Joe Gandolfo

A t the start of my career, I made a vow to myself that I would always follow up on every one of my clients every year, and that's what I do. So when I sold a $10,000 life insurance policy to a college student at Florida Southern College in my hometown of Lakeland, Florida, he also bought a lifetime service contract from me.

It makes no difference how big or small a client is. Every one of them deserves and gets the same service from me. *I service them for life.* You have to in this business. It's what separates one life insurance agent from the others. After all, there isn't a whole lot of difference in the products we sell.

After his graduation, the student entered the service, and I sold him another $10,000 policy. Then he moved to Tallahassee and worked as a page in the Florida senate. It didn't matter where he moved. I was honor-bound to keep in touch with him at least once a year. Even if he never bought another policy from me, he was my client for life. I was obligated to service him as long as his policy stayed in force.

Once, at a cocktail party he attended at a state senator's house, a guest had convulsions, and this young page, who was trained in the service to do CPR, saved the guest's life. The victim happened to be one of the wealthiest men in America, and he asked my client to work for him in one of his many business enterprises in Miami.

A few years later, this same wealthy Miami businessman (I won't mention his name because he is world renowned) was planning to borrow a large sum of money for a real estate investment. He asked my client, "Do you know anyone who has any connections with a big insurance company? I need to borrow some money."

This prompted my client to call me. "Joe, I know you are big in insurance. Can you help my boss?"

"What's the problem?" I asked.

"He wants to borrow $20 million for a real estate project. Can you put him in touch with one of your insurance contacts?"

"Yes," I answered.

"By the way, Joe," he added, "my boss doesn't want anyone locally knowing about his business. This is one of the reasons that he was receptive to my suggesting you, since you're up in Lakeland. So remember, this has to be confidential."

"I understand. That's the way I always work," I explained.

After we hung up, I made a few calls to some insurance companies. I set up an appointment for one of them to meet with the Miami businessman. Shortly thereafter, the man invited me to visit him on his yacht in Miami. That afternoon I sold him a $20 million policy to cover the loan. At the time it was the largest policy I ever sold and my highest commission. After the sale, I asked if I could use his telephone to call my wife.

When Carol picked up the phone, I said, "Honey, I'm in hog heaven."

Always take care of your small clients and be sure to give them the same quality of service that your big clients demand and get. There are three reasons that you should always give them exceptional service:

1. Every client, big or small, deserves it.

2. Small clients may someday become successful and therefore have the potential to become big clients.

3. Small clients can refer you to big prospects who can become big clients.

Joe Gandolfo is the only life insurance agent in the world to sell in excess of $1 billion in a single year. A resident of Lakeland, Florida, Joe represents several dozen life insurance companies and has clients throughout the United States. He is truly one of the legends in the life insurance industry.

SPECIAL OCCASIONS

Told by William R. Chaney

To many people, Tiffany & Company is recognized for the superior design, quality, and craftsmanship we put into our products. But when you get behind what we really do, you'll discover it all boils down to offering wonderful gifts to mark special occasions. These occasions range from a marriage to a milestone birthday or anniversary. For this reason, we like to think of ourselves as a business that makes very happy moments and marks important occasions with something of lasting value.

Slightly more than 50 percent of our sales are to customers buying for somebody else. We offer a wide selection of merchandise, ranging from a sterling silver key chain to an extraordinary diamond necklace. With so much to choose from, it is sometimes difficult for a customer to determine what to buy for a special occasion. To many customers, our suggestions are welcomed recommendations and appreciated as one of our services.

A little while ago, our corporate division was approached with an unusual request by R. J. Reynolds, one of our corporate customers. The company's vice president explained to us that he needed something unique to mark a special occasion. The company wanted to present NASCAR driver Richard Petty with a one-of-a-kind gift. After having sponsored his racing career for 35 or so years, R. J. Reynolds was looking for a gift that would express the company's high esteem for him. The gift should be one that not only showed appreciation but also would never be forgotten.

Of course, it would have been easy for us to take the vice president on a tour through the store and let him pick out something. We could have made suggestions such as "How about a beautiful crystal vase?" or "Here's an exquisite watch."

Instead, we called in our design staff, which has about 20 in-house designers. These people work closely with our account executive teams, and when their combined creative talents are put into high gear, chances are good they will come up with an elegant gift for the customer. Next our account executive set up a meeting with RJR representatives. A lot of questions were asked, and a lot of notes were taken. Then the account executive had a brainstorming session with the design staff. It was here that somebody brought up the fact that Richard Petty's trademark was a cowboy hat, which he always wore. It was a wonderful western hat that symbolized his look. Being from Kansas, I like cowboy hats too, so when the proposal came up to make an exact replica of his favorite Stetson in sterling silver, admittedly I was a little envious.

When our design staff was finished, we produced a 150-ounce silver Stetson hat. It was precise in detail. Even the boa snakeskin that surrounded the rim and the pheasant quail feathers were duplicated—all in silver. A leather band was put inside so the hat could actually be worn—although at 150 ounces, it would be quite heavy.

We put it in a display case with engraved acknowledgments listing Petty's achievements over the course of his career. When RJR presented Petty with the hat, he received it with deep appreciation.

Certainly there is a vast range of gifts in our store's inventory, but RJR would have been hard-pressed to come up with anything more thoughtful than the sterling silver hat. It's the kind of keepsake that will remain in the Petty family for a long time.

As you can see, our number-one objective was to make it an unforgettable occasion. This is the principle on which our customer relations is founded. And it is something we attempt to do with all customers who walk through our doors, regardless of who they are or what they buy. We strive to create an atmosphere that lets customers know we care about them, and that it is our desire to do something special for them. We want people to leave our store with a warm feeling and think to themselves: "That was a good experience, and something I want to do again."

I suppose it's the same feeling you get when you walk out of a truly great restaurant after having a wonderful meal. It wasn't only the food you ate that made you feel so good; it was the fine service and the way you felt because people made a fuss over you. It's the same in our business and, I am sure, every successful business—this is what makes people want to come back.

As America's most esteemed jeweler, Tiffany is renowned for its elegant, high-quality merchandise. It takes more than fine products, however, for a company to earn such an extraordinary reputation. Truly remarkable is Tiffany's exceptional service. As demonstrated in Bill Chaney's story, the company is committed to spending extra time and doing whatever it takes to make its customers happy. It is the constant effort to do more than what is necessary that develops a relationship with customers and keeps them coming back. Founded in 1837, Tiffany & Company is one of the oldest retailers in the United States. With an emphasis on providing extraordinary service to its customers, it is a company that will undoubtedly be around for many more years.

William R. Chaney has served as chairman of the board and chief executive officer of Tiffany & Company since 1984. Listed on the New York Stock Exchange and headquartered in New York City, the company operates 79 stores in 12 countries.

AFTERWORD

As the author of 35 books, I am often asked whether the excitement of writing has worn off by now. True, there have been times when I did get just a little tired with the writer's life along the way. But I can assure you that I had a ball doing this one!

The salesman in me immensely enjoyed meeting these super salespeople and listening to their favorite sales stories. In fact, writing a book like this is not exactly what I consider work. And to think I get paid for it! I deeply appreciate the wonderful people who participated in the project and so graciously shared their stories. Needless to say, without them, this book would have never been written.

Did you enjoy *The Greatest Sales Stories Ever Told?* Would you like to read *The Greatest Sales Stories Ever Told, Part II?* How would you like being in it? If you have a favorite story, send a written page or tape of it to me at the address below. Once I receive enough exceptional stories, I'll call you to conduct a brief telephone interview for details. So be sure to send your telephone number and address, along with your story, to:

Robert L. Shook
261 South Columbia Avenue
Columbus, Ohio 43209

ABOUT THE AUTHOR

ROBERT L. SHOOK is the author of more than 35 books. His books on selling include The Perfect Sales Presentation, Ten Greatest Salesperson, and Hardball: How to Turn the Pressure On Without Turning the Customer Off. A former salesman, Shook is founder and past CEO of Shook Associates and the American Executive Life Insurance Company.